Creative Dislocation—
The Movement of Grace

JOURNEYS IN FAITH

Speech, Silence, Action! The Cycle of Faith,
Virginia Ramey Mollenkott

Hope Is an Open Door,
Mary Luke Tobin

By Way of Response,
Martin E. Marty

Creative Dislocation—
The Movement of Grace

Robert McAfee Brown

Journeys in Faith
Robert A. Raines, Editor

ABINGDON
Nashville

CREATIVE DISLOCATION—THE MOVEMENT OF GRACE

Copyright © 1980 by Abingdon

Library of Congress Cataloging in Publication Data

BROWN, ROBERT MCAFEE, 1920
    Creative dislocation.
    (Journeys in faith)
    1. Brown, Robert McAfee, 1920- 2. Theologians United States—
Biography. I. Title. II. Series.
BX9225.B7617A4   230'.134'0924[B]   80-16433

ISBN 0-687-09826-2

Quotation on page 122 is from *The Lady's Not for Burning* by
Christopher Fry. Copyright © 1959. Used by Permission of Oxford
University Press.

MANUFACTURED BY THE PARTHENON PRESS AT
NASHVILLE, TENNESSEE, UNITED STATES OF AMERICA

My life has been a series of gifts. It is the nature of gifts that they are both surprising and undeserved. The worst thing—as one of my students long ago taught me—would be to be grateful and have no one to thank. Fortunately I have God to thank, but God is most present for me, and therefore most thankable, in people I have known.

To a few—among many more—who contribute to

the creative dislocation

and are thus instruments in

the movement of grace

Preeminently: Sydney
Peter
Mark
Alison
Tom

as well as: Het and Bet
Dibby and Bill
Pat and Jerry
Rachelle and Hugh
First Pres, Palo Alto
Bill and Daniel
Marion and Elie
Gustavo and Diego
Sergio and Pepo
Harle and Ken
Frodo and Sam
Janet and Ludwig
Timothy and the communion of saints

and including: some Presbyterians
most Jesuits and Benedictines
and absolutely all Sisters of Loretto

My students—at Amherst, Macalester, Union, Stanford, and Pacific School of Religion—have always tried to keep me honest and off-balance and dissatisfied. Their names, though not found on this page, are inscribed even more permanently on my heart.

Acknowledgments

Very little of this material has appeared in print before. The exceptions are portions of the "Transition," "Beauty and the Oppressed," and "Theology in a New Key," which appeared in *The Christian Century*, "The Saving Grace of Humor," which appeared in *Christianity and Crisis*, "On Making Friends with Time," which appeared in *A.D. Magazine*, and the appendix to "Maybe Small Is Beautiful . . ." which appeared in a longer version in *The Witness*. All except the first and last were written expressly for this book. The "Transition" also appeared, in an earlier form, in *Liberation Theology for North Americans*, Theology in the Americas, New York, 1978. Some of the material in "The Gift of Disturbing Discoveries" was first presented at a symposium at Macalester College in the spring of 1979.

I am grateful to members of a small reflection group that used to meet in our apartment each Tuesday morning at Union Seminary for help in refining the sections on "The Saving Grace of Humor" and "On Making Friends with Time."

Sydney and Peter, by their unyielding insistence that I be as clear as I could, thereby furnished the most important kind of affirmation, although they bear no responsibility for portions that are still either cloudy or wrongheaded.

Contents

Editor's Foreword

People inside and outside the church today are engaged in a profound revisioning of the faith journey. Wanting to honor our own heritage and to be nourished by our roots, we also want to discern the signs of the kingdom now, and to move into the 1980s with a lean, biblical, ecumenical and human faith perspective.

The *Journeys in Faith* book series is offered to facilitate this revisioning of faith. Reflecting on the social justice openings of the 1960s and the inward searching of the 1970s, these books articulate a fresh integration of the faith journey for the years ahead. They are personal and social. Authors have been invited to share what has been happening to them in their faith and life in recent years, and then to focus on issues that have become primary for them in this time.

We believe that these lucidly written books will be

widely used by study groups in congregations, seminaries, colleges, renewal centers, orders and denominations, as well as for personal study and reflection.

Our distinguished authors embody a diversity of experience and perspective, which will provide many points of identification and enrichment for readers. As we enter into the pilgrimages shared in these books, we will find resonance, encouragement, and insight for a fresh appropriation of our faith, toward personal and social transformation.

It is fitting that the first book in this series should be written by Robert McAfee Brown. In his book he shares passionately and fairly his own personal and professional dislocations of recent years, discerning the movement of grace within them. He chronicles his "loss of innocence" regarding the church, academia, some of his colleagues, and himself, with truth, humility, and his characteristic wit. His story of vocational "failure," job crisis, and an intriguing restructuring of his work style for the time ahead will provide a grid for many readers assessing their own vocational journeys. Vatican II, Union Theological Seminary in New York, Stanford University, and the liberation movements of the last two decades take Brown into issues of institutional freedom, sexism, racism, conformity. He yearns toward a liberation theology for North Americans that would turn the church inside out for the healing of this and all nations.

Pastors, laity, seminary students and faculty, college students and faculty, denominational leaders, all who seek clear focus for their own faith journey in the years ahead, will find in Bob Brown a wise and understanding companion and persistently provocative fellow pilgrim.

Robert A. Raines

Introduction:

A Self-Defensive Note About Self-Advertisement

The pages that follow are not autobiography. And yet there is a disproportionate amount of *me* in them.

This makes me uneasy.

I justify what follows as follows: my purpose is *to tell those parts of my story that may help others get a better understanding of their stories.* There is really no such thing as a solitary story; our stories involve one another. An attempt at a solitary story is minimally a pity and maximally a disaster. All stories should be solidary, and to the degree that they are, they are blessings rather than disasters.

Sallie McFague (from whom I have learned much about such matters) has written about the genre of autobiography, "We read autobiographies to find out about *ourselves*" (*Speaking in Parables,* Fortress Press, 1975, p. 146). I agree. I read about Tolkien or Marx (Groucho? Karl?) or Jeremiah,

11

not only to learn their life stories but also in order that their life stories may make an impact on my life story, telling me things about myself I did not know before.

But I would like also, without even asking permission, to reverse Sallie McFague's theme to read, "We write about ourselves in order to learn about *others*." For as I share my story, I learn new things about those who have made an impact on that story—deeper love for my friends, better understanding (I hope) of my enemies, a fuller way of seeing how we all relate to one another. If that doesn't happen when we tell our own stories, the effort is indulgent.

There is always a temptation to justify the present by reference to the *past*. I've always been chary, for example, of saving book reviews (the good ones), for fear that in moments of despondency I wil reflect, "Why not get out those old book reviews and remember how well I did?" That gets me off the hook too easily.

The opposite temptation is to justify the present by reference to the *future*. Some years ago a university library asked to become the archivist of my "papers," not only those I had on hand but also whatever I produced in the future. The offer was flattering, but I declined, worried that I might begin to think and act in the present, not for the sake of the present, but for the sake of a flattering answer to the question, How will this sentence or that insight look ten years from now? That's not all bad, and we have it on high authority that before building a tower we should count the cost. But I decided that for me it would be bad; I would be tempted to let the future censor the present, rather than letting the present mold the future. To avoid the risk of being wrong, I would be tempted to timidity "for the sake of the record."

So what follows is hardly an archivist's dream. But it is part of my dream, a dream that has been twisted and turned and a number of times almost transformed into a nightmare. It's not my full story. It is limited, roughly, to the last two decades. But it seeks to respond to the editor's interrogation, What did we learn from the sixties and seventies that might prepare us for the eighties?

So it is part of everybody else's story, too.

PART ONE:

Creative Dislocation

This book is being written during a time of dislocation that is not only geographical, but also vocational, psychic, and financial. There is a lot of pain in dislocation. I would like, on one level of my being, to stay located, to remain in one place. But I have learned that it is the nature of the Christian life to be "on journey" and I try to accept that. It's not easy.

Being "on journey" doesn't necessarily involve a change of physical location. I lived fourteen years on a university campus and went through the biggest dislocation and relocation of my life, even though my outward address remained 837 Cedro Way, Stanford, California 94305 throughout. I began those fourteen years as a fairly willing participant in what we call "the system" (a term we'll return to) and ended them in increasing distrust of almost all that "the system" represents.

After fourteen years there was a new outer location. For a variety of reasons (to which we'll also return) that didn't work, and shortly after this book is finished, I will have yet another outer location. Will it free me for a continuing journey, both inner and outer? Who knows? I will only learn in the doing. That is what is scary. That is what is liberating.

Are dislocations creative? I believe they can be. Some, of course, are destructive. But dislocation, with all its risks, is surely preferable to stagnation, which is the temptation when we cling too powerfully to what we have. When we do that, growth ceases. This is living death.

Would "relocation" be a better term than dislocation? No. It might imply that we had arrived, that the journey was over. Our location is the journey itself. But we are always being dis-located, moving ourselves or being moved (sometimes kicking and screaming) to somewhere else along the journey. It is precisely dislocation that *makes* it a journey. And it is the worthwhileness of the journey as a whole that makes the dislocation creative. Grace is the name of the movement that gives that worthwhileness.

But that is already to anticipate . . .

1

A Portfolio of Verbal Snapshots

(with a short excursus on Sacraments)

I look at a snapshot of my good friend Jordy McEntyre, age three. He is standing on a log in a field of flowers, leaning over slightly and poking a stick into a tuft of grass. Wonder is written across his face and shapes every line of his body. "That picture," I comment to no one in particular, "captures the essence of childhood."

I look at a block print Sydney made when our children were small. Several wee creatures are walking in the rain holding huge umbrellas over their heads. We see only their backsides, and yet every line of their chubby bodies tells us that they are having a ball, not only walking in the rain but experiencing the exquisite joy of walking through puddles rather than around them. "That print," I always mean to comment to my wife, "captures the essence of childhood."

I don't use the word "essence" much any more. And yet I need it now, to point at what this chapter is about. There are moments in time that capture in a fleeting second what is true of many other moments of time as well. Jordy and the chubby rainwalkers depict what we wish were always true for children—wonder and joy—and when it is not so at least we know what is missing and can search for ways to make it possible for them.

I have found it true in my own life that certain moments capture the feeling of other moments; they show in one instant something I would like to be true of other instants as well. Other moments show me up as timid or fearful or indecisive, as I do not like to be but also am. They are important moments too, and must not be obliterated from memory. Sometimes we learn more from our failures than from our successes.

All of this is what I increasingly understand the sacraments to be about. In a sacrament, life is for a single moment the way it is supposed to be in all moments. We eat bread so that Christ "may dwell in our hearts by faith with thanksgiving." We want that to be true not just when we are eating bread in church, but also when we are eating ordinary bread around ordinary tables, and when we are not even eating but just doing ordinary things—riding the subway, teaching school, making love. If Christ does "dwell in our hearts by faith with thanksgiving," then the ordinary things aren't ordinary anymore. They are special. The sacrament reminds us of what the nonsacramental is supposed to be like, so that it can become sacramental too.

So a verbal snapshot is a kind of sacrament to me—a moment in time that invests other moments of time with new meaning.

What follows is a series of verbal snapshots out of the human photograph album of the sixties and seventies.

1. photo taken with a West German pre-World War II camera in East Berlin shortly before the wall went up (May 1960).

A Lutheran church service. Only a few people are in attendance. It is no longer the thing to do. The East German Republic (DDR) has provided state alternatives for all the "religious" occasions: a name-registration in place of baptism, the *Jugendweihe* in place of confirmation, state weddings in the courthouse instead of Lutheran weddings in church. Sunday services are not forbidden, but attendance at them is looked upon unfavorably as a sign of deviation from the philosophy of dialectical materialism.

It is announced that there will be a baptism. I am amazed. Why would a young couple jeopardize their own future (as well as that of their child) by choosing the archaic ceremony when a state ceremony is readily available in the courthouse?

The couple does not have to answer my question. Their very act of bringing their baby to the church is a public statement of their priorities. They engage in significant risk because of their faith. In the face of their quiet, public courage I feel unworthy.

Later in the service I assist the pastor in the distribution of the elements. It falls on me to give the Body of Christ in the form of bread to the father and mother of the baptized child, saying to them, " . . . feed on him in thy heart by faith with thanksgiving." Who am I, who live in a relatively risk-free world, to tell them to live thankful lives in the midst of their risk-filled world?

 . . . For the first time in my life I understand, and am immensely grateful for, the ancient catholic doctrine that the efficacy of the sacrament does not depend on the moral purity of the celebrant.

2. six-hour time exposure in black and white (very black and white), at about f.90 for detail, followed by 1/1000th of a second with flashbulb.

Blacks and whites, Protestants and Jews. At this point

Catholics aren't yet into lawbreaking, though when they learn how they soon surpass us all. We are riding the buses through the South, a clergy team trying to do one simple thing—insist on riding as an integrated group of friends with nobody second-class (guess who's been riding second-class). At every bus stop we divide into teams and go into the restaurant, the waiting room, the washrooms, black and white together, insisting that as interstate passangers we are legally entitled to use the same facilities. If the local law demands segregation, we defy the local law for the sake of a higher law—*two* higher laws in fact, the federal law of the nation and the moral law of God, which in this case happily and somewhat unexpectedly coincide. I'm on the rest room detail; I'll spend four days and nights urinating to the glory of God.

It's a scary business. A bus a few weeks earlier has been burned; many Freedom Riders (as we are called) have been beaten up; most have been arrested. Any thoughts of self-congratulation, however, are quickly put aside: you think *you* are putting something on the line, white boy? think about what your *black* brothers and sisters are risking.

We've had twenty-four frightening hours. Most of the assault has been verbal but some has been physical, and the threats mount the farther south we go. We get a six-hour respite in Sumter, South Carolina, and we are in a black Baptist church until the 10:30 P.M. departure of the next bus south. We are dog-tired and more frightened than we'll admit behind our clerical dog collars. What are we doing here anyway? It's only going to get worse.

Around suppertime, folks in the black community of Sumter gather to feed us—who needs clerical words of institution at such a time?—and after supper we have a service in the sanctuary. We are fed again, this time filled with the power of the Spirit, whose mysterious, brooding, universal presence is mediated through local people and thereby pinpointed for a few moments in the "negro section" of Sumter, South Carolina, with unbelievable intensity . . .

It is now very late the same night. We have left Sumter without incident. The local police, hating our guts, have seen to that; they want no "episodes" within the city limits.

I am very, very tired. I doze fitfully, nourished by our earlier hymn-singing and praying, but frightened by the recollection that we will have to "integrate" the Savannah, Georgia, rest rooms at 3:30 in the morning. Lulled by the steady movement of the bus, I am almost asleep. The bus slows down dramatically. The change of rhythm causes me to sit bolt upright. We have entered a town. I look out of the bus window and see a long procession of hooded figures in sheets lining each side of the street. My reaction is immediate: the Ku Klux Klan is stopping the bus they're going to get us in the dead of night   Sydney   honey   I love you.

1/1000th of a second later I come to full consciousness. I am gazing at rank after rank of freshly painted parking meters.

3. 1/50th of a second flash, which is just about how long it took a few previously rigid clerics to get turned around.

Rome, Vatican II. Protestant "observers" are having an off-the-record discussion with a few Catholic *periti* (theological experts to the bishops). The exchange has been open, frank, and rather heavy. A priest suggests that we conclude with "The Our Father," a big ecumenical gesture in 1963. Not only a big ecumenical gesture but a big ecumenical problem as well, because Roman Catholics emphatically stop after "but deliver us from evil" (*sed libera nos a malo,* as we say in Rome), while Protestants go on rapidly with "Forthineistheking-domandthepowerandthegloryforeverandever."

We come to the crucial parting of the ways. There is a perceptible "imperceptible pause."

Then:

Protestants: (emphatic silence)

Catholics: Forthineisthekingdomandthepowerandthe
gloryforeverandever.

Protestants and Catholics together: AMEN!

We look at one another amazed. Without any cue, each of
us has operated out of sensitivity to the tradition of the
other. A new day.

Gus Weigel, doughty Jesuit, finally decides the euphoria
has lasted long enough. "Why shouldn't we say the final
doxology?" he almost growls. "It's nothing but a Catholic
addition to the original text."

**4. box camera exposure on coarse-grained film that
makes enlargement difficult.**

1965? 1966? 1967? It doesn't really matter, save that it
was during the Vietnam years. Davie Napier, dean of the
chapel at Stanford University, and I are driving to San
Francisco. To speak at an anti-war demonstration in Kezar
Stadium? To march with our own wives in a protest action
down Market Street? To lock arms in front of a draft board
office so as (illegally) to impede entrance? It doesn't really
matter, save that any of those occasions could have elicited
the wistful thought from one of us: "Won't it be *great* when
all of this is over and we can finally get back to studying
again the way we used to?" Who says it? Davie? Bob? It
doesn't really matter. It could have been either one of us,
since both of us almost simultaneously realize that *it will
never again be the way it was before. Never.* The verb "to study"
will have a new definition. It will include such things as
driving to San Francisco to engage in some kind of action, as
a way of taking the "study" seriously.

Clear gain.

Even if initially accepted rather grudgingly.

**5. 1/100th of a second, i.e., long enough to arrest the
action, while the Special Branch of the South African
police, clearly visible outside, are wondering if there is
enough action inside to warrant an arrest.**

Headquarters of SWAPO, the black activist student movement in Durban, South Africa. My wife and I are talking to Steve Biko, a rallying point for black consciousness in South Africa until the police murder him, after which he becomes a rallying point over which they have lost control.

Steve Biko is not impressed with us. Why should he waste his time with two white liberals who will leave and try to state his case for him to other white liberals? After all, he continues in almost surly fashion, that's why the black-consciousness movement has begun in Africa—because white South Africans are presuming to speak for blacks and determine what is good for blacks. Who needs more of that?

I am nonplussed. How can I respond to this angry young man? But Sydney is not nonplussed. He has struck a responsive chord in her. "I think I know what you mean," she replies. "At home, when men speak on my behalf as a woman, or explain to the world just what it is that women 'really want,' I feel frustrated and even angry."

Steve Biko's angry face relaxes. He cannot suppress a smile. The wall of separation between us has been overcome. A *rapport* has been established across cultural, racial, class, and sexist lines.

The real conversation begins.

6. negative from a large panoramic camera capable of photographing eight hundred people—but from the rear, so their faces will not be discernible in case the police get possession of the plate.

Lima, Peru, 1977, in the midst of a "summer course" for lay people on theology in the church today. Tame, safe stuff up North. Dynamite down South. Theology, we hear, is a matter of reflecting from a Christian perspective on what one is doing in the world to transform social structures for the benefit of the poor. Since it is the poor who are in attendance, they are getting marching orders. But they know that to agitate for change will put them at odds with all the authorities.

The talk subsides. The plea for social transformation is over. Now there will be a eucharist. Tame, safe stuff up North. Dynamite down South. The Mass begins. We take part freely, welcome at the Lord's Table of our Catholic friends.

"The Mass is over." We sing a hymn to conclude. Not just any hymn. This particular one is the Magnificat, attributed to Mary, a lovely, spiritual person, as we all know, the humble handmaiden of the Lord. Tame, safe stuff up North. Dynamite down South. For the humble hand-maiden of the Lord turns out to be the greatest rev-olutionary of them all. The *real* marching orders come straight from her. The police cannot stop a bunch of Catholics from singing a hymn by the Blessed Virgin. But listen to the words: I had never really heard them until that day.

God has scattered the proud in the imagination of
      their hearts,
God has put down the mighty from their thrones,
and exalted those of low degree;
and has filled the hungry with good things,
and the rich God has sent empty away.

The humble handmaiden of the Lord has set the agenda for the next half century of Christian activity in Peru.

7. twenty-four-second time exposure, at 2 A.M., that seems to last for eternity.

A South American airport departure lounge. Many soldiers throughout the airport, guns on the ready. Standard operating procedure. The letters we are taking to Costa Rica for friends who did not dare put them in the mail are safe in a large brown envelope deep within the suitcase I am carrying. We have decided not to put them in the checked luggage since it may be opened without our knowledge; nor do I want them on my person in case there is a physical check. We make it through customs, breathing unaccustomed sighs of relief.

But tonight there is one more check point than usual. Relief turns to surprise.

The suitcase is opened, the large brown envelope extracted. Surprise turns to fear.

The large brown envelope is opened. Fear turns to terror.

The letters themselves are extracted. What is there to feel beyond terror? If the letters are opened, my friends are dead and I have betrayed them.

After a moment the inspector shrugs, puts the letters back in the large brown envelope, and returns the large brown envelope to the suitcase. He had been looking for dope. He makes that most infinitely beautiful of all human gestures, an upraised thumb, which means "okay."

I rejoin my wife, whose pounding heart during this brief, interminable episode, has been reverberating throughout the entire airport complex. "Jesus Christ!" I breathe to her as I sit down. I'm not sure yet whether it was a prayer or a curse.

For twenty-four seconds of one early morning, we experience the reality with which our sisters and brothers in Latin America live during the twenty-four hours of every single day and every single night.

8. exposure data lost since I forgot to advance the film and two images were superimposed on the same negative.

Tuesday morning: A small group of us are listening to a recording of Ralph Vaughan Williams' *Sancta Civita,* a musical rendition for multiple chorus and orchestra of the final triumph of the Holy City. I cheat. I look ahead in the libretto and note that there will later be a chorus celebrating the fall of Babylon, symbol of the evil forces threatening the Holy City. I anticipate how Vaughan Williams will score the exultant theme: double fortissimo, maybe even triple fortissimo,

trumpets, timpani, cymbals. What a climax it will provide!
I have it wrong. Vaughan Williams is a better theologian
than I. The chorus is *pianissimo,* and although there is
recognition that evil has been conquered, there is no wild
exultation. The price has been too high for wild exultation;
there are too many wounded, too many dead, there has
been too much devastation. The rejoicing must be muted.

Thursday evening, same week: A large group of us are
listening to a lecture by Elie Wiesel on the book of Joshua.
This time I cannot cheat for I do not have a script. He tells
us that for years he has postponed coming to terms with the
book of Joshua, since it contains so much bloodshed, so
much vindictiveness, so may battles. And besides, he
complains wistfully, it doesn't have any poetry.

We hear the story of the book, retold as only Elie Wiesel
can retell it, with all the bloodshed and all the vindictiveness
and all the battles.

And so, he concludes (and I paraphrase), I am glad there
is no poetry in the book of Joshua. For poetry should never
be used to glorify brutality, beauty should never be
employed to justify ugliness. We may sometimes have to
fight, even to kill, but let us never exult in our killing even
for a noble cause. The price is too high for wild exultation;
there are too many wounded, too many dead, there has
been too much devastation. The rejoicing must be muted.

**9. occasional snapshots with a variety of exposures on a
variety of films from a variety of cameras over the course
of two decades:**

There we all are at Ft. Cronkite Beach: Mark and Alison
are looking for carnelians with Sydney, while Tom and
Peter are throwing sticks for Hugo to retrieve, or (an earlier
photograph) running away from the waves with Fridgie,
whose canine comportment forbids her getting wet (in
another incarnation Fridgie was a highly fastidious white
Russian princess) . . . There we all are a few hours later,

enjoying espresso at Sausalito . . . Those four shots of four faces and four guitars are (successively) Peter, Mark, Alison, and Tom, learning to play and sing the music appropriate to each of their own tastes . . . There are Peter and Mark (hassled by their draft boards because they won't fight in Vietnam) leaping for joy as LBJ announces that he will not seek reelection . . . There we all are, gathered around the crèche on Christmas Eve, putting the animals and the wise men and the shepherds around the baby who is a small center of sanity in a large and crazy world . . . That's Tom, with the beautiful guitar he made himself from scratch; Peter, on the business end of the camera with which he captures life and humor and wonder and religious depth on film; Mark, bending over the plate from which a lithograph will come, capturing a symbol we otherwise would miss; Alison, organizing Harvard to fight apartheid in South Africa and economic exploitation in South America; and Sydney, challenging stereotypic job patterns through New Ways to Work in Palo Alto and Project Work in New York City and a whole host of other projects (she's the one on the left, the *far* left, asking, "Why not?" instead of "Why?") . . .

Many snapshots, many moments, many memories, as we fan out into the world, but continue to affirm a family base from which we go and to which we return, not only for sustenance, but for fun.

10. 1/5th of a second, hand-held camera, against the side of a bus, so that the print is mercifully blurred.

Returning from a debilitating downtown meeting shortly after my fifty-eighth birthday, I fight my way onto a crowded #5 bus, reconciled to standing throughout the exhausting sixty-eight-block ride to 122nd Street. As I find a pole against which to lean my weary body, a young girl of eleven or twelve stands up and offers me her seat . . .

Never before that moment have I thought of dyeing my

white hair back to its original brown, or exploring the possibilities of a face-lift, but I do think more than fleetingly about such deceptions during the torturous ride that follows that lovely and devastating gesture.

11. exposure data not on file, but indelibly recorded on the film of memory.

The dining room table, 711 McGiffert Hall, Union Theological Seminary. Bread and wine on the table. "The Peaceable Kingdom," a bas-relief by Alison of the lion and the lamb lying down together, hanging on the wall.

We have come into the dining room after hearing four Roman Catholic women tell us about a meeting of two thousand Roman Catholic women in Baltimore discussing the role of women in the church. Their conclusion: there is nowhere to go but up. They are discouraged and hopeful.

It suddenly seems important that the moment around the table be more than an ordinary moment. Canonically and liturgically we are separated from one another at the Lord's Table. At least we should not be separated from one another at this human table. I say something to that effect and we pray together.

Without benefit of clergy, without an act of consecration that would be canonically acknowledged, the four women who have been at Baltimore distribute bread and wine to the rest of us, and it is indeed "the bread of life" and "the cup of wholeness." We are nourished, restored, healed. There is a real presence. For a few moments life is as it is meant to be—everybody included, no one excluded.

The peaceable kingdom.

12. 1/100th of a second at f.8 (it's a gray, cheerless day), encapsulating a moment four thousand years old.

The roof of the crematorium at Birkenau, the death-camp of Auschwitz. We are standing on ruins the Germans tried (unsuccessfully) to obliterate, to hide evidence that six million Jews had been shot and gassed and burned in such places, solely because they were Jews. I reflect: if Golgotha revealed the sense of God-forsakenness of one Jew, Birkenau multiplies that anguish at least three and a half million times. For the rest of my life, this crematorium will represent the most powerful case against God, the spot where one could—with justice—denounce, deny, or (worst of all) ignore God, the God who was silent.

Of what use are words at such a time? So many cried out to God at this spot and were not heard. Human silence today seems the only appropriate response to divine silence yesterday.

We remain silent. Our silence is deafening.

And then it comes—first from the lips of one man, Elie Wiesel (standing in the camp where thirty-five years earlier his life and family and faith were destroyed), and then in a mounting chorus from others, mostly Jews, the great affirmation: *Shema Yisroel, Adonai Elohenu, Adonai echod,* Hear, O Israel, the Lord our God, the Lord is One.

At the place where the name of God could be agonizingly denied, the name of God is agonizingly affirmed—by those with most reason to deny. I shake in the tension between my impulse to deny and their decision to affirm.

Because of having stood *at Birkenau,* it is now impossible for me to affirm God in the ways I did before.

Because of having stood at Birkenau *with them,* it is now possible for me to affirm God in ways I never did before.

2

From Jerusalem to Athens and Back Again:

A Chronicle

The early church was in a constant flap over the question, "What has Jerusalem to do with Athens?"—Jerusalem symbolizing faith, devotion, and the community of believers, Athens symbolizing the pagan world of reason, detachment, and nonbelief. Could they be related? Could faith and reason share anything in common? Could pagan and Christian inhabit a common world? Tertullian, one of the early church fathers, favored ideological divorce and answered with a resounding, no!, while the Apologists opted for ideological cohabitation and found many ways of saying 'yes.' The debate has raged ever since.

I've lived a lot of my life in Jerusalem: child of the manse, church upbringing, summer conferences, seminary, ordination, a life of preaching and teaching. After teaching two years at a church-related college in Minnesota I returned to my alma mater, Union Theological Seminary, and

spent nine years working up from instructor to full professor
with tenure. At forty I was Auburn Professor of Systematic
Theology, firmly launched on a professional career in
Jerusalem.

Two years later I forsook Jerusalem and moved three
thousand miles to Athens, to teach religious studies at
Stanford University. Henry P. Van Dusen, then president
of Union, never understood such folly on my part: Union
was not a place from which one departed, it was *the* place to
which one hoped to be invited. And I was throwing all that
away.

The decision was not easy. But I had been unsure for a long
time about whether I belonged in Jerusalem. I had a concern
about those whom Schleiermacher called religion's "cultured
despisers" (partly because on one level I have always been one
of them myself) and wondered if the theological enterprise
could survive constant exchange with such people. Furthermore, I did not want to be a narrow "specialist." I realized that
I would rather introduce college sophomores to Bonhoeffer
and Buber and see their worlds come alive, than supervise
three-hundred-page doctoral dissertations on a single nicety
of the thought of either of those worthies. In addition, as far
as Stanford was concerned, I felt a debt. The position was
open because a close friend, Lex Miller, had dropped dead at
breakfast the spring before. We had done our doctoral work
together at Union; indeed, we had shared together the high
point of our academic careers, passing the German exam.
Lex had grown a tender plant at Stanford, initiating a
Program in Religious Studies, and it still needed watering.

After months of vacillation, I finally accepted the Stanford
offer, excited and attracted by the challenge of trying to be a
theologian in Athens, even though family, colleagues,
friends, and possibly even foes, thought I was quite balmy.

On the day of my official appointment by the Stanford

Board of Trustees, as I figured out later, I was in jail in
Tallahassee, Florida, charged with "unlawful assembly with
incitement to riot" for sitting in the airport lobby at the
conclusion of our "Freedom Ride," waiting for the coffee
shop to serve an integrated group of ministers and rabbis. It
never did. I have often wondered what the Stanford
Trustees (not best known for far-out social concern) would
have done had they known my whereabouts that day.

But whatever second thoughts they may have had later
on about my presence on their campus, once the appointment was official and public, I had none. I stayed at
Stanford fourteen years and must count the first ten of
them the best years of my life. Once we were settled in, the
family became enthusiastic; the kids loved it, and Sydney
began to carve out a life of her own, of which there will be
more to say later. Classes went well. I got a degree of
affirmative response that increased my own affirmation
both of my subject matter and my students. My faculty
colleagues and I grew from a "Program" of three to a
"Department" of eight. My presence at two sessions of the
Vatican Council as a Protestant observer gave me special
entrée to Roman Catholic students, not to mention the
Roman Catholic community in the Bay Area, California,
and the entire nation. During the Council years I spoke
widely in Catholic churches and on Catholic campuses,
wrote for Catholic publications, and Sydney and I formed
deep friendships with many priests and nuns. When the
post-Vatican II upheaval began, our home became a kind of
halfway house for dozens of them, some of whom stayed in
the church, some of whom left, and with all of whom we
discussed, prayed, and agonized.

These were also the civil rights years. I remember one
particular moment of truth in an ethics class when I was
lecturing on what we then called "the race problem"—as
Selma was erupting. It was clear to me that I ought to be in
Selma in solidarity with black sisters and brothers, rather

than in Stanford engaging in talk. I went. Probably the students learned more by my abrupt departure than they would have learned by my continuing presence. I certainly did, and learned to boot that I have no instinctive taste for martyrdom.

During this time Vietnam was intruding into our national consciousness. It refused to go away, and from about 1964 to 1973 it was the dominating reality of my life. I have elsewhere (in *The Pseudonyms of God*, Westminster Press, 1972) recounted my pilgrimage from occasional mild concern to ongoing acts of civil disobedience. I paid no heavy price—two arrests and a few days in jail—but I was constantly dealing with people, my students, who were facing not "a few days in jail" but up to *five years* in jail for their unwillingness to fight in a war they considered immoral. They sensitized me, and I, with them and on their behalf, tried to sensitize the upper middle class to which their parents belonged. I wrote widely, spoke all over the country, and tried to do my homework on the politics of Southeast Asia.

The fact that Peter and Mark became draftable during these years was crucial to my thinking. On the one hand, I was torn between not wanting them to have to fight in that kind of war (or any war), and yet not wanting to impose my views on them. On the other hand, I was immensely glad and reassured as it became apparent that they, too, felt the war to be wrong, and had arrived at their own decisions not to fight in it. Their independence was clearly asserted: at the first Stanford "sit-in" I publicly urged students not to participate; walking over to the building that was occupied (despite my advice), I got a friendly wave from Peter who was standing on the roof.

I had not wanted my sons to be put on the spot of paying penalties for *my* beliefs, but when it became clear that they were acting out of *their* beliefs, a strong family solidarity

developed. Peter had a two-year hassle with his draft board,
papers going back and forth between California and
Washington—appeals, new appeals, statements, new statements, rebuffs, new rebuffs, were the order of the day.
Mark, three years younger, was going through the same
process when the fighting overseas finally ended. Sydney,
too, was deeply involved in anti-war activity with local
community groups, through many projects, marches,
petitions, and campaigns, and had as sustained an
engagement as any of us. Alison and Tom, though younger,
were with us on many marches and demonstrations, and
had to struggle with their younger friends (and sometimes
their teachers), some of whom insisted that anti-war activity
was unpatriotic, even as others gave them strong encouragement.

Another moment of truth: in 1966–67 I received a grant
from the Danforth Foundation for two quarters of
interdisciplinary study to make me a more knowledgeable
citizen of Athens. I enrolled in a course in computer
science, and also one in advanced biology taught by Donald
Kennedy, a faculty colleague I particularly admired. After a
few weeks, however, the invitations to speak and write
about Vietnam were increasing to the point where I had to
choose between wholehearted academics for six months or
wholehearted anti-war activity for six months and God only
knew how much longer.

I made the latter choice. Better, the choice was made for
me as the horror of what we were doing in Vietnam
continued to unfold. I cannot begin to communicate the
anger, the despair, and the helplessness we felt during
those years. I was visited by the FBI and refused to
cooperate with their interrogation. After all, they were only
out to get me. In response, Bill Keogh, on the faculty of the
Law School, organized a legal defense committee against

the day I would be federally indicted, which we all expected.

Actions on campus mounted, and I found myself in a real bind. I didn't want to give mixed messages, and I felt that to be against violence in Vietnam and yet engage in violence in California was a very mixed message indeed. Thus, I was not trusted by the "radicals," who frequently wanted our endless anti-war rallies to escalate to local violence ("trashing" was the word), nor was I on congenial terms with most of the "liberals," who wanted peaceful protest but no peaceful protest that involved civil disobedience. As things got worse, however, people's attitudes changed, and we had one extraordinary day in 1971 when every draft board in the Bay Area was simultaneously blocked by students and faculty in a coordinated nonviolent effort. One group, including Peter and Sydney and myself, kept the San Mateo Draft Board shut down for three days, because the police didn't want to arrest "respectable" faculty, clergy, and students. There were no such compunctions in Berkeley, however, when Peter and I joined a group there on Good Friday, preaching a Good Friday sermon, as we put it, "on the pavement."

Throughout this time I never got a single hint or plea from any member of the university administration that I should "cool it." Many of them disapproved of what we were doing, but there was still enough sanity in a mad world for them to realize that freedom of expression and conscience is something that universities exist to maintain and defend. I am grateful to Stanford for the freedom it gave me, particularly since it enabled me to say and do things that professors in small colleges and pastors in small congregations could not have done without getting fired.

I had little temptation to think of myself in heroic terms; others—a few in the public eye, but most doing the important work without public recognition—were light years ahead of me in the degree to which they put themselves on the line. But I did have new corners of my being opened up, as I anticipated court, prison, and separation from my family. After losing on the Coffin-Spock indictments, government officials clearly chose to stop prosecuting protesters. So there was no long separation. It's about all I feel like thanking the government for during those years.

So the Stanford years were eventful and productive, both in teaching and in relationship to the outer world. They came to an end. I left. And now, four years later, I live half a block from the campus where I worked for fourteen years. As I walked past old haunts for the first time after being back in the area (here's where the class on theology and literature met, there's where the White Plaza rallies were held, here's where I really flubbed a student question, there's the pulpit from which I preached about the Christmas bombings), I wondered if nostalgia would overwhelm me with sadness that I had left. And I made an important discovery: we can accept that the past is nonrepeatable. I learned much during those fourteen years, but I am not living those years any more. I have been able to let them go with a lot of gratitude, some disappointment, but no trauma. I'm lucky. It is best not to keep reliving past decisions, or to try to get back to "how things were before." Embrace the new.

The return forced me to ask again, however, What went wrong? Why did I leave? Why, finally, a return to Jerusalem?

My place within the Department of Religious Studies changed slowly, subtly, and definitively. I believe, and continue to believe, that the most creative teaching grows out of the commitment of the teacher to the importance of his or her subject matter. That I was a "believing Christian" was to me an asset in trying to communicate what Christianity is all about. It would have been a liability only if I had demanded similar belief from my students—a demand I explicitly disavowed at the beginning of every course I ever taught. I pledged that I would be as fair to all other positions as possible (I was a very persuasive apologist for Albert Camus). So long as my perspective was known to the students, and I did not pose as "neutral" (a teaching impossibility, I believe), I felt that academic integrity was safe. Increasingly, however, my colleagues came to feel that objectivity, detachment, and phenomenological description were the only appropriate stances for teaching religion. We had a simple, basic, clear, and acknowledged disagreement. When I was about the only one left who felt that an explicit faith stance was appropriate, I had a choice: either to continue as a "loner," an anomaly in an otherwise coherent program, or look elsewhere. For other reasons as well, I began to look elsewhere.

My appreciation to Stanford for protecting my freedom of conscience and expression remained, but it began to be balanced by a recognition that Stanford and places like it were part of the huge military-industrial-educational complex that was not only supporting the war but profiting from it. Research in some areas of the sciences was contributing to the war, Defense Department contracts were helping support other departments, and many members of the Board of Trustees were associated with industries lavishly rewarded for designing or making instruments of human destruction. Stanford, I came to realize, could tolerate a certain amount of offbeat protest without any fundamental challenge to its place in our society. It would not, nor would other universities, become a catalyst for social change. Its role would increasingly be that of a conserver, a very good one, of the status quo. Was that institutional direction the one I wanted to endorse with my own future?

Two events demonstrated that Stanford and I were going in opposite directions. A tenured English professor, Bruce Franklin (a "self-avowed Maoist" as the newspapers always described him) was involved in a number of anti-war actions that were felt by the administration to go beyond the bounds of conduct appropriate to a professor, and the university initiated charges against him. I was a member of the seven-man advisory board charged to hear the case. It was a backbreaker. We worked six hours a day from early September until early January, with only Sundays off and a couple of days at Christmas, in addition to our regular teaching schedules. (That all seven marriages survived those months is a minor miracle, or maybe a major one.) The end result of the hearings was a five to two recommendation for Franklin's dismissal, the chairman, Donald Kennedy, and I being the two minority votes. We both felt that some form of censure was appropriate, but agreed that dismissal was too severe. The majority, of course, prevailed with the Board of Trustees, and Franklin was fired. I was, and remain, very worried about the inhibiting effect of such an action on freedom of speech on university campuses, and I was shaken by the action of the university.

A more immediate reason for my own departure was the refusal of the university to grant tenure to a colleague in Religious Studies. Professor Jerry Irish came to Stanford with a Ph.D. from Yale. We taught together, had congenial theological concerns, and became close friends. In the course of four years at Stanford, two of his three children died, one after a lifelong illness, the other totally unexpectedly within twenty-four hours while the Irishes were with a Stanford student group in Rome. These events, needless to say, seriously intruded into the "scholarly production" he would otherwise have completed, but the university ruled that even so he had published too little. Two ironies compounded the decision: (a) several years earlier he had been the initial recipient of a new university Gores Award for Outstanding Teaching, and (b) the day he received word that his appeal had been denied, the senior class asked him to speak at their commencement exercises as one of the three professors who had meant most to them during their four years at Stanford. There was even a Catch 22: having been told a year earlier that he must get some things published if he were to be granted tenure, he decided to play that game and did—a book, two articles in learned journals, several book reviews all appeared within the year, after which spate of production one of the administration officials stated publicly that he was always suspicious of people who published a lot just before they were up for tenure . . . Joseph Heller, where were you when we needed you?

I was very angry, and remain angry, at the treatment Stanford gave Jerry, and his dismissal clarified for me that my own future belonged elsewhere; I was not only at theological odds with my departmental colleagues (though we were for the most part good friends), but I was increasingly at odds with the university as a whole, both on its posture toward the world outside and on its view of the kind of people it needed for its own future.

But where to go? A strange thing had been happening downtown on the corner of Kingsley and Cowper. Our family's experience in the First Presbyterian Church on that location had been so rewardingly positive that I was increasingly persuaded that there was a future for institutional Christianity after all, and that the parish church could still be a vital force in people's lives. Training people to replicate situations like "First Pres Palo Alto" would not be a bad use of one's time.

So I had already begun looking from Athens back toward Jerusalem. The move to Athens had been right in 1962. Perhaps now it was time to return to Jerusalem, utilizing what I had learned in Athens. For a year, I had the good fortune of being able to sample both worlds. Thanks to my friend Davie Napier, who had become president of Pacific School of Religion at Berkeley, I was invited to teach there half-time for a year, with the possibility of a future full-time appointment. So for a year I taught on both sides of the Bay. I have almost bucolic recollections of the P.S.R. experience. The students were exciting, and I was teaching things that meant a lot to me—ecumenical antecedents of liberation theology, theological implications in the writings of Elie Wiesel, theology as narrative.

And then . . . out of the blue came an invitation to return to Union Seminary and teach Ecumenics and World Christianity. This precipitated the toughest decison Sydney and I have ever made. Four years after the fact I still do not have full perspective on it, and considering the fact that it didn't work out (I resigned within fifteen months of my return to Union) I probably never will. But for whatever help it might be to others who face similar vocational traumas, I will reflect briefly on the dynamics of the coming to, and going from, Union.

I had an enviable problem—a decision between teaching at two first-class seminaries, both located close to great universities, both very ecumenical in their outlook. Union had fallen on some hard times (so the public story went) and was now in process of rebuilding. And although I was excited by my time at P.S.R., I felt an institutional loyalty to Union (I had also done my B.D. degree there) that was probably the deciding factor in the decision. In addition, the post of Ecumenics and World Christianity seemed tailor-made for my own developing concerns. There was a tremendous tension, however (to indulge in understatement), in asking Sydney to leave the work she had been doing in Palo Alto out of New Ways to Work, the vocational agency she and a few other women had created. That was a bit offset by Union's offer to let us work together as "codirectors" of a new Ecumenical Program. That, too, was important in our final decision, but unfortunately we left the details of how a codirectorship would work for later negotiation. That was a mistake.

After having weighed the offer for six difficult months, we finally accepted, persuaded, I believe, that there were too many good possibilities in the "new Union" to turn the offer down.

We went through a tumultuous uprooting from fourteen years of friends at Stanford, and made the three-thousand mile-trek back east with hearts heavy at what we were leaving and hearts excited at what lay ahead.

It didn't work.

It was soon clear to me that I was in the wrong job at the wrong time in the wrong place.

1. The basic reason it didn't work, I believe, is that I thought zeal could go bail for expertise. "World Christianity" was where my passionate concern had come to lie. But passionate concern, I soon discovered, is a different thing from being the one member of a graduate faculty responsible for Asia, Africa, Latin America, the Middle East, and everything in between. At fifty-six, I was in a new area of professional responsibility, and by the time I could even minimally have mastered it, my five-year contract would have run its course. The terms of staying on would have been to fake it. I didn't want to fake it.

2. In addition to teaching, the job called for an immense amount of administrative skill. My greatest administrative skill in twenty-five years of teaching had been an ability to avoid tasks calling for administrative skill. I didn't know the first thing about it. It was taking 80 percent of my time, even with some assistance. This was a bad use of my time and a bad use of the seminary's resources. Enough said.

3. The biggest personal frustration, subordinate to the two substantive points just made, but still important, was the fact that the structures at Union simply had no way to accommodate a husband and wife as genuine *co*directors of anything. What had looked in anticipation like an exciting new concept in job-sharing turned out to be one more situation in which the wife was welcome as an assistant, but

could in no sense be an equal, since the structures of decision-making and voting were limited to faculty members only. Her opinions could be voiced only through me—a frustrating arrangement for two people trying to work as equals. This was both a deep disappointment to us and a discouraging commentary on institutional life in the 1970s.

4. It was clear, in other words, that Sydney and I had wrongly assessed Union's priorities, just as Union had wrongly assessed our priorities. We soon discovered that we were at very, very different places, and I must try to sort them out, not to attack Union, but because I think what happens in one institution is a kind of case study in what is probably happening in other institutions.

Our own increasing dissatisfaction with "establishment values" had led us to hope that Union (where that dissatisfaction had earlier been nurtured for both of us by Reinhold Niebuhr, John Bennett, and others) could move institutionally with some disregard for "establishment values." We did not realize with what vigor Union's policy makers had chosen to move away from participatory democracy within the Union community. We had hoped that Union was ready to take genuine risks for the sake of educational innovation, whereas the policy was clearly to reclaim earlier educational models. We had hoped that Union would be looking for ways to make some kind of major institutional identification with victims of oppression both in New York City and the Third-World, whereas the policy seemed clearly designed to concentrate (though not exclusively) on a mission to main-line Christians. We had hoped that Union would stress "World Christianity" for the marginated and exploited peoples of the world, whereas the policy, while open to the study of "liberation" concerns, was clearly designed to keep that permanently "balanced" by other, less threatening options. I personally had hoped, indeed expected, to recover the excitement of working together with faculty colleagues sharing a common vision—an excitement that had disappeared at Stanford. For whatever reasons, I didn't find it. A handful, yes, and perhaps that should have sufficed. But most faculty had their clearly set-out personal agendas—fair enough—and they were miles away from mine. (After a meeting where the goals of a possible ecumenical program were presented for reactions, I commented to an old and trusted friend, "On a scale of 1 to 10, I would put faculty enthusiasm at about −3." "Oh no," he responded, "that's much too pessimistic. I'd put it at about +3.") It could be responded that the appropriate response would have been to stay and *build* support, however slowly and painstakingly. Fair enough . . . over a fifteen-year haul. I had only five.

So what Union did not realize in rehiring me, and what I did not realize in accepting an appointment, was how much we had both changed in the intervening fourteen years. Maybe Thomas Wolfe is right and you can't go home again. At all events, I had gone down the road of "reluctant radicalization" (which I will discuss later), and Union, seeking to recover from what it considered the "onslaught" of the sixties, seemed more interested in recovering the stability of the fifties than exploring radical options for the eighties.

If time should prove that assessment incorrect, no one will be happier to eat his words than I, for I continue to believe that a place like Union could be the scene of a unique adventure—not only insisting on "academic excellence," but determining to be an intentional Christian community open to new leadings of the Spirit in the area of patterns of work life, relations to staff, use of building facilities for the wider community, communal economic disciplines, and less beholdenness to the principalities and powers of this world.

Despite whatever disappointments and disillusionments there had been along the way, however, we left Union on an

upbeat note, thanks to support from a handful of faculty
(who will know who they are) and a wonderful sense of
rapport with a whole armload of students, along with good
friends in other parts of the city—far-seeing friends at New
York Theological Seminary (doing the most exciting things
in theological education anywhere), beleaguered friends
fighting the bureaucratic battles at the Interchurch Center
with pluck and courage, high-minded friends struggling in
local parishes, deeply committed friends engaged in the
wider "secular" battle to make New York City a more
human place to live. But mention of the students is the most
appropriate way to close this chapter of our lives. They were
magnificent—supportive of us and our dream, hard-work-
ing on the projects we shared, angry and indignant along
with us at certain events along the way (notably the
seminary's reluctance to promote Beverly Harrison to full
professor without a lot of pressure), and responsive to the
people to whom we felt responsive, such as Dorothee Soelle
and Gustavo Gutiérrez, with whom we found ourselves
sharing a political-social-theological vision that remained
decidedly in the minority. What we learned from and with
them made it all worth it—the dislocation involved in the
decision to go there, the increasing momentum of realizing
we didn't belong there, the trauma of coming to terms with
that miscalculation, and the decision to leave. The students
taught us many things in those three years. I hope we can
put them to good use.

3

Three Reflections
on the Chronicle

The above pages are the bare bones of two decades of movement and change. The story has a lot of "lessons" in it that still elude me, and I do not intend to scrutinize it with too homiletical an eye. But I do want to offer three initial reflections on the chronicle, dealing, respectively, with motivation, transformation, and clarification.

1. Motivation: I love, therefore I protest

There is a lot of protest in the chronicle—protest about racism, the war, the university, the seminary, the church. One of the things I learned in the first decade, when the Protestant-Catholic dialogue began to be central for me, was that *pro-testari* means "to testify on behalf of . . . in the name of . . . for the sake of . . ." The connotations are positive, not negative. Negations arise out of affirmations, not the other way around. To be a Protestant, I learned, and tried to teach, was not to be *against* Catholics, but to be *for* the authority of Scripture, the priesthood of all believers, and a host of other affirmative convictions.

This positive connotation of protest was often lost in the sixties, sometimes by the protesters but more often by those who disapproved of the protesters. "Why so negative?" they would ask. "Why are you *against* so many things?" Many people failed to understand (or we failed to make clear) that to be against the use of napalm was based on an affirmation that since Vietnamese had eternal worth in God's sight, they should have immediate worth in ours, and that incinerating them was therefore wrong. Many people failed to understand (or we failed to make clear) that to be against America's war policy in Southeast Asia did not represent hatred of America, but was rather the expression of a desperate love for America, an agonized awareness that what we were doing was not only destroying Asian bodies (and American bodies) but our national soul as well. We were in effect appealing from America's propensity for blindness to America's capacity for vision; from a petty view of our national destiny to a more ample one. I spent the better part of one summer writing a long introduction to a book then published by Clergy and Laity Concerned About Vietnam, cataloguing the many "war crimes" *our* troops were committing in Vietnam, acts of atrocity that contravened all of the international conventions for rules of warfare to which we as a nation were both morally and legally accountable. We called the book *In the Name of America,* and the title was the clue to our intention. We could have called it *In the Name of Decency,* or *In the Name of Judaeo-Christian Morality.* But we didn't. We were challenging what America was doing precisely "in the name of America," trying to point out that our own heritage had the resources to recall us from such folly, and that we were besmirching our name, our honor, our history, our sense of who at our best we feel ourselves to be.

In the pledge of allegiance we affirm ". . . liberty and justice *for all*" (italics added). Usually we don't take the italics very seriously. Usually we mean, ". . . liberty and justice for *us*," or ". . . for people *like* us," but not necessarily for Vietnamese or Chileans or South Koreans or women or blacks. But "liberty and justice *for all*" (italics retained) is the America dream at its best. When we turn the dream for all into a nightmare for many, it is an act of love and patriotism to note the distortion, loudly and even raucously if necessary, in order to tilt the balance from nightmare back toward dream, so that the dream can become reality.

So war protest was motivated for us out of a sense of loyalty, not disloyalty, as an attempt to recall to our national compatriots who we *should* be, in contrast to the baleful reality of who, for the moment, we actually *were*. The protest was out of love for our country, our own people, the Vietnamese people, and the possibility of a decent world. When love sees its intentions being destroyed, it has no recourse but to issue a warning cry and oppose those things that threaten love's survival and victory.

I love, therefore I protest.

2. Transformation: the stigma of being a "liberal"; or, the road to reluctant radicalization

Having to take seriously that protest is an expression of love leads to the development of a healthy paranoia. There is so much around that seems deliberately to contravene love.

The "liberal" option I understand as the assumption that things are basically in pretty good shape, but that we can and should do a great deal of tidying up around the edges. As liberals, we don't need to challenge the structures of our society; all we need to do is democratize them a little more, or spread their benefits a bit more widely, so that more Jews or blacks or women or Chicanos or _____ (insert

name of currently oppressed group) are included. It was
my operative assumption for years.

I was very defensive about being a liberal in the early
sixties. The so-called "radicals" on campus were scornful
of "the (expletive deleted) liberals." "Give us consistent
conservatives any day," they said. "At least we know where
they stand and the issues can be joined."

I now believe their assessment was fundamentally
correct. My present inability to accept the basic structures of
our society as truly just is a bequest from minority peoples
who have forced me to see that although the system works
to *my* benefit, it works against *theirs*. It is a system in which
the rich get richer while the poor get poorer, in which 6
percent of the world's population (the USA) consumes 40
percent of the world's resources. That's an immoral statistic
and an immoral fact. It means that structures that benefit us
destroy others. And although we can perhaps close the gap
a bit (say from a 6/40 ratio to a 9/37 ratio) there is *no way* that
those with influence and affluence are significantly going to
share power or let their position of manifest superiority be
challenged. The liberal belief that a system based on
ruthless competition is somehow benign to losers, doesn't
work for me any longer. So for me there is now in the
eighties a stigma attached to being a liberal far more
significant than the pejorative use of the term in the sixties.
The liberal option is *now* saying something like this to me:
"Let us use all our skills of rhetoric and earnestness to
defend as just a system that is in fact unjust, that guarantees
things to us it must thereby necessarily deny to others, that
promises mammoth rewards to a minority of exploiting
white go-getters at the cost of increasing misery to a
majority of exploited nonwhite victims."

The road from there to radicalization (i.e., getting to the
radix or root of the problem rather than dealing with
surface manifestations) is "reluctant" simply because I am
as envious of my own creature comforts as the next person

and tend to search as assiduously as anyone else for reasons to justify keeping what I have. Only reluctantly do I acknowledge that I am the perpetrator of a con game against the majority of the human family (and ultimately against myself as well, since if my actions demean the humanity of others, they demean my own humanity as well). Since I don't eagerly initiate changes in the structures, it is fortunate for the cause of justice that the victims of those structures are forcing people like me to see the world through their eyes and confront the demand for change.

I am helped in that direction by the "healthy paranoia" referred to above. "Just because you're not paranoid," the bumper sticker says, "doesn't mean they're not out to get you." I'm not so concerned that "they" are out to get me as I am that "they" (which finally means "me") are out to get all the weak, poor, defenseless people of the world and keep them that way. They do it with smiling faces, pinstripe suits, and elegant prose. I've become particularly paranoid about the facades of fashionableness and conformity and good grammar; Mobil Oil ads are a particular anathema—tones of earnest reasonableness, dripping with folksiness, employed to make absolutely sure that whatever happens to the rest of the human race, Mobil's profits continue to soar. So "healthy paranoia" I would define as acknowledging that whoever it is they are out to get, they will explain it in ways that sound as though they were doing their victims a favor.

When I finally got a copy of my FBI dossier under the Freedom of Information Act, I learned a lot about my country and about human nature, most of it paranoia-inducing. One thing was how many thousands of dollars my government had spent trying to entrap people like me, and how many hundreds of thousands of dollars it had therefore spent going after the people it finally indicted (Dan and Phil Berrigan, Liz McAllister, Bill Coffin, Benjamim Spock, and others). And I also got a new insight into human nature, Presbyterian-style; I learned that after I

had spoken on the floor of my presbytery about Vietnam, a
fellow presbyter had informed the FBI that a traitor was at
large in the San Jose Presbytery and the cops had better get
a move on. The unveiling of this patriotic solicitude by a
brother in Christ came as a shock to me; I had always
supposed that the feds infiltrated such gatherings incognito
and collected their own data. I don't know whether that was
"healthy" paranoia or not.

3. Clarification: on being able to afford to fail; or, when grace is least apparent and most needed

The above chronicle can also be read as a series of
apparent successes that gradually turned into failures:
things that started out well somehow went sour. The
three-year interlude at Union seems particularly to have
had the smell of failure hovering over it. How does one
cope with failure, real or apparent?

One way is to challenge the definitions we commonly
attach to the terms *success* and *failure*. Were the three years
at Union a "failure" because I didn't complete my five-year
contract and realized that I could not fulfill the assignment I
had been called to fulfill? For most of the second and third
years I thought so, and my inner life was a raging torrent of
remorse, disappointment, bitterness, and anger. But I now
begin to realize that a lot of foundation work was laid,
mostly by Sydney along with students and good friends, and
that a successor will have a lot on which to build. Many of the
things we initiated are being picked up and developed by a
lot of students, a few faculty, and some friends, all of whom
will see to it that the concerns are kept alive.

But even if not, even if one puts the most negative
reading on those three years, I draw strength and
perspective from Christopher Fry's comment, "The Christian is one who can afford to fail." Assume the worst:
assume that all that happened in the three years at Union
was that some important mistakes were made. That would

at least alert a successor not to repeat them and might free the way to move more rapidly into positive alternatives. On those terms, my contribution would not have been in vain. I can "afford to fail," since something good will be resurrected out of my failures, thereby rendering them other than simply failures. And grace has a lot to do with that.

Grace means that there are two further consequences. One I would describe by the phrase, "little deaths, big resurrections"; by this I mean that a personal disappointment or miscalculation, a "little death," can be the occasion for a "big resurrection," the emergence of new possibilities, new hopes, new life, in ways far beyond our calculation or miscalculation. It happens all the time: some unexpected and creative use is made of something we diffidently offer, and the realization that it is so comes as a pure gift. We discover that although grace did not seem apparent it was still there, transforming for good what we were fearful had only been for ill. Joseph's brothers, so the book of Genesis informs us, meant evil against him, but God meant it for good (Gen. 50:20). What we do can be picked up and used in ways beyond our intentions or even our imaginations. Surely it's worth three years of life to discover that.

The other consequence of being able "to afford to fail" is the discovery that we never do anything alone; not only do *our* actions always have consequences for others, but *others* can pick up and use and complete whatever it is we have initiated. The "results" may be the work of other hands than ours, but in this we can rejoice. There is indeed a "communion of saints"—some living, some dead (and it doesn't finally matter very much which)—who surround us. I illustrate this by a symbolic configuration: Father Abraham, Brother Dietrich, and Sister Luke. That is a communion of saints if there ever was one! Brother Dietrich, who a generation ago put everything on the line against the Nazis, and thus empowers us to put a little more on the line today against contemporary enemies; Father Abraham, who had to flee an actual tyranny in Poland in the thirties, and was thus sensitized to do battle with a potential tyranny in America in the sixties, thereby lifting us out of a quasi-complacency in which we might have remained without his authoritative presence (Jahweh, if an anthropomorphic god, surely looks like Abraham Heschel); and Sister Luke, who fought all the internal battles for *aggiornamento* in the Roman Catholic Church and then turned with equal vigor to outside battles for human rights, racial dignity, and just about everything else, thereby helping the rest of us see that if she, a spry youngster of seventy-five, can keep struggling, maybe we oldsters in our fifties and sixties can do the same.

Two men and a woman (no way to get equal time for both sexes out of the number three), a Catholic, a Protestant, a Jew, two Europeans, and a North American (or two North Americans and a European, depending on which decade you choose), champions of the dispossessed—they could all be said to have been failures, or at least less than smashing successes, since the causes for which they live and die are never secure and any victory can always come unstuck.

But I am left with a splendid query: with "failures" like that, who needs success?

4

Look Out,
Your Globe Is Shrinking:

or,
Larger Horizons, Smaller World

In my original outline, this was to be the longest
section since it propounded the central theme. In the actual
execution, it has become one of the shorter sections,
because although it still propounds the central theme, that
theme has spilled over (as all central themes should) into
other sections as well. So let us focus some rays that are
shining with diffused light elsewhere.

The biggest *dislocation* in my life has been the discovery
that the perspective I have entertained most of my life is too
narrow, parochial, and class-oriented to do justice to what is
going on in the world. The dislocation has been *creative*,
however, because once the original trauma of discovery has
been faced, it is beneficial to discover that one's perspective
"is too narrow, parochial, and class-oriented to do justice to
what is going on in the world." It frees one up to seek—or be
given—a perspective that is less narrow, less parochial, less

class-oriented, and therefore does more justice to what is going on in the world.

I tried in *Theology in a New Key* (Westminster Press, 1978) to deal with ideology (which is what I am talking about), as a perspective we impose on our world, often unconsciously, so that what we think we perceive will conform to what we want to find. An old trick.

For a long time my perspective included a belief that the spread of the American influence was beneficial not only to America but to its recipients, that white people had a real concern (I mean a *real* concern) for the welfare of black people, that those with power were willing to share it when asked, that if we occasionally "intervened" in the affairs of other nations it was always for their own good and at considerable cost to us, and that the viewpoint from which I reached all of these insights was unbiased and open. In actual fact most of the insights were spawned by my own desire to have them true, and I often (as I now see) filtered information carefully to make sure that nothing threatened such convictions.

All of them have gone on the discard heap. So have a lot of others.

What has happened is that I have been privileged to have some living contact with people who look at the world from a different perspective, and they have demonstrated the inadequacy of mine. I have been fortunate, within the space of a few years, to visit some troubled spots in the world, rather than just read about them. (I was never west of Chicago until I was twenty-five.) In my twenty-sixth year I saw what was left of Nagasaki (it took the U.S. Navy to get me west of Chicago) and experienced the bitter fruits of the "war effort" I was supporting as a navy chaplain. At the Uppsala Assembly of the World Council of Churches, which I attended as a delegate in 1968, I had my first extended contact with people from the Third-World, i.e., those nations seeking to avoid commitment to and thereby dependency on, either the USA or the USSR. I was already deep into anti-Vietnam activity, but it was important to discover that my perceptions of the havoc we were wreaking in Southeast Asia were shared by Southeast Asians (and Africans and Europeans and Japanese and Indians and Latin Americans . . .) as well as by white liberals in North America. In 1972 Sydney and I spent three weeks in South Africa as guests of the Presbyterian Church of Southern Africa. Thanks to the Presbyterians we traveled widely, met a significant variety of people and mixes of people, felt at firsthand the despair and fear in all hearts, and discovered that South Africa was the entire global scene writ small—same tensions, same imbalances of race and power, same sense of helplessness, but geographically concentrated with an unbelievable intensity, and shouting some lessons not only about South Africans but about ourselves. In February 1975, I was a delegate at the WCC meeting of the Fund for Reconciliation and Reconstruction in Indochina, held in Vientiane, Laos, and preceded by five unbelievable days in Phnom Penh, Cambodia, only a couple of weeks before it fell, unbelievable to discover that beautiful land being wasted and destroyed, largely because we had initiated actions precipitating their own civil war. In November of the same year I was an adviser to the fifth assembly of the WCC in Nairobi, Kenya, and gave the keynote address on the assembly theme, "Jesus Christ Frees and Unites." I gave about three-quarters of the speech in Spanish (quaking in my boots) to try to symbolize the need for English-speaking delegates to disavow the "linguistic imperialism" that always dominates such assemblies where 90 percent of the business is done in English. The decision to do so was impulsively reached a few months earlier as I was returning from a Detroit conference of "Theology in the Americas," at which about twenty-five Latin American theologians had had to speak English to us for a week. I was embarrassed by this and resolved to turn the tables around, even if ever so slightly. I am glad I stuck with the decision, for although a lot of people were irritated and a few people were outraged, the Latin Americans embraced me (literally and metaphorically) afterward for even this minimal acknowledgement of who they were. This was worth all the icy editorial rebuffs from *Christianity Today* and its camp followers. Perhaps nobody remembers what was said, but that it was said in Spanish seems to have been remembered. The year 1977 provided a chance for Sydney and me to spend three weeks in Latin America (Peru, Chile, Argentina, Costa Rica, Mexico) and ten days in Cuba. Although my platform Spanish (painstakingly rehearsed) was several cuts above my conversational Spanish (almost nonexistent), we nevertheless got an extraordinary exposure to radical priests and brave laity who were putting everything on the line to make the gospel's "preferential option for the poor" a reality in the life of the church. Three weeks in Bangalore, India, in the summer of 1978, at Faith and Order meetings of the WCC, provided another kind of "conscienticizing"; I learned at firsthand how desperately certain European theologians resist the attempts of Third-World delegates to introduce liberation themes into an ecumenical document. All these impacts from afar were strengthened by impacts from near at hand. I have already noted the significance for me of Peter's and Mark's resistance to the draft, and our hope that such choices wouldn't have to confront Tom when he reached eighteen. But there was also the conscienticizing for all of us of the year Alison spent in Chile after her graduation from high school, just after the *coup* brought Pinochet and his assassins to power. Alison encountered at firsthand, and managed to communicate to the rest of us who remained at second hand, things we knew intellectually but could not have internalized as well without her help: not only "torture of political prisoners" but also the inability of her own Chilean family to get enough food;

not only "repression" but also friends forced into hiding and friends betrayed by informers.

I include this fact-filled recital (in the longest paragraph I have ever written) only to suggest the variety of experiences and their intertwining, as they have left their impact upon me.

The impact? Very clear. The larger the horizon becomes because of such experiences, the smaller the world turns out to be. I once knew in general terms that we are one human family, and that what happens in one place affects all other places. Now I know it in specific terms: the young Steve Biko who was later murdered; brave white South Africans now under indefinite "house arrest"; a Cambodian army officer who wanted to be a farmer and is now surely dead; the middle-European delegate at Nairobi who could only talk in whispers about life in his country, looking over his shoulder between every sentence; the incredible bravery of Latin American Catholics fighting ugly regimes; the freed-up feeling of Cubans who have successfully toppled an ugly regime. These, and many others, drive home, kindly but relentlessly, "The USA claims to be our friend [the Cubans don't say that and with good reason] but you are destroying us. Your businesses, your government, your CIA, your military, all support the repressive regimes that are the sources of our harrassment, poverty, torture, and death. Can't you work at home to change the policies of your country?"

Having finally discovered that we are meant to be one human family, I also discover that one of the reasons we are *not* one human family is laid at our own doorstep: we use our power not (as our rhetoric claims) to help others out of poverty, but to enhance our own wealth. Our use is abuse.

Yes, my globe has shrunk. Yes, I now have a larger horizon. But I don't like the view.

What can I do about that?

As I was dismantling my study in preparing for our

three-thousand mile physical dislocation, I was intrigued by the pictures (in addition to family) that had made it onto my study walls and stayed there. Along with a large map of South America, there were four portraits: Dietrich Bonhoeffer, Elie Wiesel, Dom Helder Camara, and Gustavo Gutiérrez. One Protestant, two Catholics, and a Jew. They are among my reminders of our shrinking world, and if I am truly to respond to the way I now know that world, it is through their eyes that I must look, it is to their voices that I must listen, and it is (this is harder) to their lives, attitudes, and commitments that I must look for the modes to emulate and embrace.

My task—our task—is clear: to engage in a quantum leap from being a "voice for the voiceless" (a role I now realize is patronizing) to moving over so that the voiceless can not only have space on the platform but also get control of the mike.

5

A Marriage Paradox:

More Centers, Deeper Centering

It would take a whole book (one that I would like to write some day with Sydney) to deal with changing perceptions of marriage and families in the sixties and seventies. Included here are some fugitive themes that would find their way into such a volume.

Let me begin with a wide perspective. I think the marriages that made it through the sixties and seventies (as well as those that didn't) have to be seen in relation to the upheaval of the times, since they could not avoid being challenged and threatened, and then either broken or deepened, by what was going on.

We were lucky. Ours deepened.

To make the point involves challenging a widespread assumption. It goes: the sixties were a time of outreach and social engagement; the seventies were a time of inwardness and privatization; the task of the eighties will be to bring those concerns together. I have no quarrel with the characterization of the sixties or the proposal for the eighties. I do have a quarrel with the characterization of the seventies, for it seems to me to be based on sexist assumptions from which we need deliverance.

What I have learned in retrospect about "the activism of the sixties" is that it was (with some brilliant and important exceptions) a very male-oriented activism. The men were in the foreground, marching, demonstrating, going off to Washington, getting attention and getting arrested; the women were in the background, doing a lot of the organizing and a lot of the local marching, but sharing neither excitement nor headlines, fated mainly to absorb pain and fear, not to mention neglect by their male activist friends. (The exception was when the women could be "useful" to the men. The campus cry, "Chicks up front!" in the early days of police confrontations was predicated on the assumption that, as the language of the moment put it, "pigs would not beat up on chicks," so the presence of women meant that the men had a buffer between themselves and the billy clubs. When it was discovered that billy clubs were no more respecters of sexual differentiation than of persons, the willingness of chicks to remain up front noticeably and rightly diminished.)

What I am learning in retrospect about "the apathy of the seventies" is that it was a very male-oriented apathy. The seventies were the time when men stopped marching, demonstrating, and getting arrested. But (and it is a large and crucial *but*) the seventies were also the time when the women's movement came into full self-consciousness, and there was a level of *feminine* "activism" beyond anything our human history has ever known—writing, marching, meeting, lobbying, organizing, legislating, conscienticizing. If it was a different activism from the sixties it was activism none the less, and probably of a sort more conducive to long-range results than that of the preceding decade.

Conclusion: there was a "retreat" in the seventies, and it was a male retreat; there was also an "advance" in the seventies, and it was a feminist advance. I hope that in the eighties we can put our two acts together, and that rather than passing one another by as we advance upon, or retreat from, the barricades, we can join together in a common assault on the most obvious citadels of injustice, recognizing that as long as they threaten either men or women they threaten both.

From that wide perspective, let me now focus on what it all meant for families, specifically for our family. I covered my tracks above by noting that the insights there stated came to me "in retrospect." I wasn't thinking that way ten or probably even five years ago. So I have a lot about which to repent in relation to the times I was even close to the firing line in the sixties. My family paid the real price. However unconsciously I did it, I surely communicated a sense that there would be something a little ignoble in their wanting husband and father home more often, when he could be out slaying those dragons, or holed up writing treatises on dragon-slaying.

For middle-class, moderately liberal, male types, there was undeniably a kind of "kick" in being arrested and jailed. It did some acknowledged social good, but it also filled some less acknowledged individual existential needs about guilt, male identity and "relevance." And it surely brought no "kicks" to the families. They were left to wait, to worry, to interpret it all to their friends, to contact lawyers, to receive angry phone calls. On one important occasion—the Good Friday draft board action in Berkeley—Peter and I were arrested together. But such things were the exception rather than the rule. The men got the glory, such as it was, and the families paid the price. I don't feel very good about that. In retrospect.

The combination of activism and teaching and lecturing and writing and traveling meant that I was away from home a lot. I justified some of it on grounds that we couldn't make it without the extra income—which was true, we couldn't— but it meant that I missed a lot of my children's growing up, and they had more than their share of what is now called "single parenting." And I am just very lucky, luckier than most, that somehow (by grace, if I'm pressed for an explanation) we have survived all that, and with whatever hard times we may have individually and collectively gone through, Peter, Mark, Alison, Tom, Sydney, and I are now at a point where we not only love, but like, one another, sharing ordinary moments in a way that makes them special moments. I have no recipe for how that happened, but I do have some advice: listen to one another, and cherish the family moments while you have them; they will be gone before you know it.

It is more difficult to write about Sydney's and my life together. The intimate details of that life together belong to the two of us alone, as long as we both shall live, and I have no interest in exploring them publicly. But some parts of our mutual conscientization are of more than private interest, since they reflect changes through which many other couples (and single people) went, and are still going.

One need not have read between the lines of this book to notice that through our early married life Sydney and I fit the roles for which society had conditioned us—the male breadwinner, the female homemaker; the man stepping out, the woman staying home; the masculine paid employee, the feminine unpaid volunteer. A lot of decisions had to be made in terms of my job—where we lived, for example, and (to some degree) how we spent our time: if I had a seminar on Thursday evenings we didn't go out with friends on Thursday evenings, and if the seminar was held in our living room (which it usually was), the kids needed to be elsewhere and quiet. To be sure, we had control over who our friends were and what we did with our own time, and Sydney had her own interests quite apart from and in addition to all of the above, but to a significant degree much of life gravitated around the dictates of my job.

For a while it worked pretty well. It meant that even New York City apartments could be called "home," and it was fulfilling for all of us. Sydney cherished the magic of childbearing and childrearing. She says that with conviction to me, and I believe her; she says it with even more conviction to friends who are temporarily soured on childbearing and childrearing, and I believe her even more. So, no regrets there, only affirmations—though I do concede (in retrospect . . .) that I could have pulled more weight in the kitchen, the diaper-washing and other childrearing aspects of those years. Sydney, I am sure, would have conceded that at the time, without the need for retrospect at all.

As the children grew older and Sydney had more time at her disposal, a new factor began to influence how we related (a) my job, (b) our family, and (c) her outside interests. For those outside interests, necessarily very part-time when the children were small, increasingly came to focus in an area where she had accumulated considerable professional expertise. She now has a professional center of her own, and the result has been that her new professional center and my ongoing professional center, rather than driving us apart, have actually been drawing us closer to each other. Today there are multiple centers in our life together, but the more we develop them, the more they overlap. Creative dislocation. How has this happened?

Her focus has been work life—how the jobs people do can be fulfilling rather than destructive for them and for society, how people can work together cooperatively rather than competitively, how decent work can create a decent society, how new patterns of work (job-sharing, part-time work with benefits, and the like) can free people up rather than tie them down. She helped start an organization in Palo Alto, called New Ways to Work, that was interviewing

three thousand people a year when she left, and she has had
a central hand in creating another work-oriented group in
New York City called Project Work. She has written more
foundation grant proposals with her colleagues than any
group of human beings should have to write, and she knows
things about restructuring work patterns in small businesses and larger ecclesiastical hierarchies that will contribute to long-range quiet revolutions far more effective than
most of the short-lived noisy ones.

Now that might seem a far cry from my theological
interests, and my theological interests might seem a far cry
from Sydney's nitty-gritty grappling with specifics of daily
life. The opposite has been the case. She has had to think
about work from a theological perspective, and I have had
to think about theology from a work perspective. Those
dealing with theology had better have a concern for the
nitty-gritty; those dealing with the nitty-gritty had better
reflect on the ultimate meaning of the nitty-gritty (which I
offer *gratis* as a new, spontaneously arrived at, definition of
theology). So we've had a chance to keep each other honest
as we ply our separate trades together.

We've begun to share our findings with others and learn
from the feedback such occasions generate. A key occasion
was the invitation from Pacific School of Religion to give the
annual Earl Lectures at that institution *together*. This
imaginative gesture (thanks mainly to Joy and Davie
Napier) forced us to develop some dialogically constructed
material around the theme "Can the Rat Race Be
Redeemed? Toward a New Theology of Work." We have
since been refining this material in joint lectures in places as
diverse as Tallahassee, Florida; Kansas City, Missouri;
Youngstown, Ohio; Sherman, Texas; Louisville, Kentucky;
and Abiquiu, New Mexico. Sooner or later it will be a jointly
authored book.

All of that has been new and exciting. The catch (there is
always a catch) is that so far the sharing has had to be done

more in the occasional on-the-road appearances and in our private life together than in the day-to-day structuring of our professional lives. Indeed, one of the issues with which our lectures are having to grapple is the reluctance of institutions to be open to new patterns of employment. I have already described our disappointment at being unable to work out genuine job-sharing at Union, and need not repeat it here. But by the end of the third year we had developed a way of working together in spite of the structures rather than because of them. There was an appropriate recognition of this at the closing Communion Service of our final year, when the seniors are empowered to invite "a faculty member" to preach. The seniors used their empowerment to defy convention; instead of asking "Professor Brown" to preach, they asked the two of us to do a dialogue sermon.

Sooner or later, the structural decisions will begin to reflect on an official level what is happening on an unofficial level at the existential cutting edge of institutions. I just wish it didn't take so long.

All of which may sound as though things have gotten awfully "professional" in our relationship. So let me close on a different note. In the foreword to *Theology in a New Key*, I expressed gratitude to "Sydney, for the fact that her own liberation struggles are being carried out with a grace that has deepened, rather than threatened, an already specta-cular marriage." Two years later, I have two regrets about that statement: one, I wish I had put it in italics, and two, I wish I had added, "Sydney, honey, I love you, and not just when the Klan is breathing down my neck."

6

Beauty and the Oppressed

There is beauty and there are the humiliated. Whatever difficulties the enterprise may present, I would like never to be unfaithful either to the one or the other.

> —Camus, *Lyrical and Critical Essays*, pp. 169–70, who speaks of "the humiliated," where I choose (I hope in faithfulness to him) to speak of "the oppressed."

Heath, Massachusetts. It is the moment before dawn. I sit and watch a landscape come alive. Shapes emerge out of nothingness (creation all over again), slowly transformed from strangeness to familiarity. Trees, stones, a wall, a chipmunk. *Two* chipmunks. Silence, blessedly invaded by a white-throated sparrow ("Oh Sam Pea-body come to tea . . ."). Finally, the sun enflames the highest point of the

maple tree that towers over the lesser pines. How
wonderful to be alive.

And yet . .

During the very moments when I am enthralled by the
unfolding of a summer morning, people whom I respect
are denied such pleasant options; either that, or they have
rejected them for other options.

I reflect—in the harsh light of day now—that at this very
moment Diego is organizing in steamy Chimbote, that
Gustavo is struggling with the poorest of the poor in the
Rimac slum of Lima, that Pepo is . . . well, better not say
what Pepo is up to, or even which of many Pepo's I mean,
since what they do on behalf of the oppressed in their
oppressive countries frequently lands them in prison.

How can I bring these two worlds together? Diego and
Gustavo and Pepo 1, Pepo 2, Pepo 3, Pepo 4 are entitled to
beauty. And I have an obligation to the oppressed. I am not
entitled only to sunlight; they are entitled to more than
darkness. So I yearn for a way of living that can be
responsive to, and is described by, both the slow movement
of Beethoven's string quartet, Opus 59, No. 2, and also the
plight of the farm workers in the Central Valley of
California; that can find resources to create a new synthesis
of reflection and action in both the beauty of the
"Archduke" Trio or the "Waldstein" Sonata and also the
oppressed of the *poblaciones* of Santiago de Chile.

It is not an easy task. I think I know a little about what it
means to speak of "oppression" even though I have seldom
experienced it. But I know very little about what it means to
speak of "beauty," even though I have frequently experienced it. (It's a bind similar to the one St. Augustine got
caught in over the concept of time. He knew what it was, he
reported, until somebody asked him to explain it.)

The dictionary gives some help: directly ("the quality or
aggregate of qualities in a person or thing that gives
pleasure to the senses or pleasurably *exalts the mind or spirit*"),

and inadvertently ("a particularly *graceful,* ornamental or excellent quality"). "Graceful," grace-filled. A good start.

I'll go beyond the dictionary by proposing that we need not equate beauty with "something attractive." Whatever "exalts the mind or spirit" can be an instance of beauty. I have already cited dawn and chamber music. I want also to include artistic creations as occasions for the introduction of beauty where there was no beauty before. They too "exalt the mind or spirit."

My family has been important in sensitizing me to this awareness. It is a wonder and a joy to me that Sydney and I have nurtured a collection of artists. Apart from a very unprofessional love of music, I am a goner when it comes to such things as sketching, sculpting, or crafting, though I love creating things with words. So most of our children's artistry comes from her. All of them keep me in touch with a world from which I tended to drift away during the sixties and early seventies—a world to which they (and a few choice friends) now continually call me back. Peter with his photographs, Mark with his lithographs, Tom with his jewelry-making, Alison with her drawings of the immortal "Corporal Fox," Sydney with her sketching and block prints, my sister Betty with her movies, all keep a part of me alive that might otherwise go stale if not dead. I'll go the dictionary one better: they not only "exalt the mind or spirit," they exalt my mind *and* spirit.

But there is always a temptation to become so enthralled with the creations of that world (all of them analogues of God's creation) that we diminish or ignore or even shut out the other world, the world of oppression. It's good, every now and then, to withdraw in order to gain perspective; it's bad if the withdrawal threatens to become permanent. And sometimes it does. That's not a putdown of the creators of beauty but a comment on how we appropriate their beauty.

Let us come at the problem from another kind of beauty. Not long ago I visited Beth Hatefutsoth, the museum of the diaspora in Tel Aviv, Israel. It includes a constantly changing projection of color transparencies of Jewish faces—youthful faces, sad faces, smiling faces, bearded faces, Polish faces, Lithuanian faces, faces of Hasidim, faces of holocaust survivors, old faces, gnarled faces. Seeing them truly "exalts mind *and* spirit" (we're going to keep one step ahead of that dictionary definition) with the glory of the human venture as well as its debasement. And what I discovered was that the beauty in those faces had nothing whatever to do with whether or not they were "attractive." The faces that most exalted *my* mind and spirit were the old faces, the gnarled faces—the faces of those who had been through upheaval, dislocation, hardship, oppression.

Oppression . . . In those old and gnarled faces, beauty and oppression came together. Not beauty because of oppression (that spawns ugly theories that "justify" oppression). But, quite simply, beauty in the midst of oppression, beauty despite oppression, beauty that not even oppression could liquidate, suggesting that the dichotomy "beauty/the oppressed" may not be ultimate and might even be false. That's a clue: maybe *all* kinds of beauty have clearer implications for the world of oppression than I have realized before. So much those Jewish faces taught me.

At the very end of this book I intend to explore that clue further by looking at one more Jewish face. But before doing so, I need to probe other ways of relating beauty and the oppressed. Although I've hardly arrived at a satisfactory theory of aesthetics, here is where I have gotten so far:

First, last, and always, *beauty is a good in and of itself,* quite apart from any "utilitarian" value it might have. It is a gift, to be affirmed simply for the fact that it *is,* whether it serves any immediately useful purpose or not. I am entitled to glory in the summer morning or the quartets of Beethoven or the creations of my children sheerly for themselves.

With that firmly (if swiftly) nailed down, we can note that *exposure to beauty sometimes has functional results.* Sometimes,

in the midst of a struggle, I discover that it is the memory of
the sunlight or the quartets or the Brown creations that
keeps me going. Furthermore, the sunlight of *any* morning
is to be cherished not only for the beauty it reveals, *but also
for the ugliness it exposes,* an ugliness that might not even be
visible apart from the sunlight. (That's also a parable, the
exegesis of which I leave to readers.) A world in which
beauty dwells should not be a world in which anyone
experiences the ugliness of oppression, but a world in which
all can embrace beauty freely because none are oppressed.
Even the recognition of beauty can be a call to action on
behalf of those to whom beauty is denied.

In stronger terms: *beauty can be enlisted on behalf of the
oppressed.* There is a danger in propagandistic art. And yet,
alongside the classic *Ars gratia artis* (art for art's sake) I want
to emblazon an escutcheon that reads *Ars gratia justiciae* (art
for justice' sake). Consider an extraordinary fact: beauty
came forth from the concentration camps. Pictures were
painted, poems were written, sculpture was created . . . by
the inmates! The resultant beauty is certainly not "attractive"; most of it is gruesome, but in a strange and powerful
way it does "exalt the mind and spirit," for it speaks both of
the indomitable courage of mind and spirit on the part of
Jews who might simply have crumbled, and also serves
today to enlist our minds and spirits in continuing
opposition to the defilement it so tellingly portrays.

Beauty can be enlisted on behalf of the oppressed.

. . . But never the other way around: *oppression can never
be enlisted on behalf of beauty.* If we have the strength to do so,
we can volunteer *our own* pain or sorrow or oppression for
the creation of a beauty that will shock and challenge but
ultimately exalt the mind and spirit, as did Elsa Pollak
(Auschwitz #A-5170) or the children of the Theresienstadt
concentration camp. But we can never enlist the pain or
sorrow or oppression *of another*. Elsa Pollak can decide to
make creative use of her anguish, Beethoven his deafness,

van Gogh his poverty, James Agee his despair, but we can neither demand that they do so, nor propose that concentration camps or deafness or poverty or despair are somehow justified if beauty follows in their train. Even to whisper such a proposal is to justify oppression in the belief that something good might come of it. Our task is always to eliminate the oppression, never to exploit the oppressed.

Elie Wiesel, worried (as we saw earlier) by the vengeance present in the book of Joshua, and complaining in addition that "it has no poetry," is finally grateful that poetry has not been employed to glorify vengeance. Beauty, he remarks, must not be enlisted to justify the un-beautiful. Pablo Casals, shocked by totalitarianism in his native Spain, refused to play the cello there during the Franco regime, and the thundering silence of his noncompliance remains to this day a witness to the incompatability of indulging our own beauty while remaining oblivious to someone else's oppression.

Camus is right: relating beauty and the oppressed presents "difficulties," and we have scarcely broken the ground around the problem. But surely tilling that soil is one of the most important things we are put on earth to do.

I have discovered one other thing about beauty and the oppressed. But I want to save it till the end . . .

7

Transition:

A Handy Summary of Lessons Learned in the Sixties and Seventies, for Those Who Like to Read and Run Simultaneously as They Enter the Eighties

1. It is important to get on record as opposing evil. It is also important to be effective in stopping evil. But if you can't stop it, at least oppose it. It is even possible that in ways you cannot foresee, your attempt to get on record can be effective, although it is somewhat easier to do this in the USA than in Argentina. Remember that "results" can almost never be measured. Backup consolation: at the very least, things might have been even worse if you had done nothing.

2. You mustn't be too picky in choosing allies, but you must also be willing not to keep them too long. You can easily be co-opted (being the token "liberal" in a group with other ends in view for which you will later be held accountable), but if you opt out of such situations in order to remain "pure," you get nothing done at all.

In looking for allies, never count too much on the

institutional church. Individuals, yes; small groups, yes; but rarely the institution as a whole. Be very open to working with secular Jews who still have prophetic passion in the marrow of their bones, probably inherited from their grandfathers, who always turn out to have been rabbis.

Common cause can be made with people who have a variety of motives. There will be counterparts in the eighties of the student who wants to save his skin, the businessman who has decided that war is bad for business, the pacifist who feels that all wars are wrong. Be prepared for the fact that such alliances may be very temporary; tomorrow you may need to be on the opposite side from all of them.

3. Although you must keep some priorities about what is really important, remember that almost all issues centering on social change are interconnected. You may originally have thought that for those in the civil rights movement to become involved over Vietnam was diversionary; but you probably came to see that the draft was drafting twice as many blacks proportionately as whites, and that there was a racial and genocidal component to what we were doing to dark-skinned Asians. Issues for the eighties (disarmament, challenges to nuclear energy) will have similar interrelationships.

The word here is "holistic analysis."

4. A variant on #3: try to be clear who the enemy is. It is likely to be the case that politicians are more beholden to the Trilateral Commission than the other way around. Don't settle for the luxury of individual enemies. My discovery has been that the whole system is the enemy. My earlier analysis was too political and too little economic. I am discovering that when the fundamental analysis is economic, that goes a long way toward explaining the politics.

5. The escalation of moral numbness demands the escalation of moral protest. In the sixties, as yesterday's unthinkable act became tomorrow's accepted practice, more radical protest was called for. The big step was over the line of lawful protest into nonviolent civil disobedience. At the time it was a huge step; in retrospect one wonders why it did not come earlier. That tended to diminish in the seventies. It may be needed more extensively in the eighties, especially as big business puts its weight behind nuclear energy that can destroy us all.

6. Further probing of #5: as a technique, nonviolence can be useful; as an ideology it can be dangerous. The unquestioned success of nonviolence in certain situations in the sixties often suggested that it could be successful in all other situations. But proposals to urge nonviolence on all Third-World peoples, or on all minority groups at home, can be irresponsible, just as egging them on to violence can be irresponsible. White ministers arrested in nonviolent civil rights demonstrations might not be worked over in jail; blacks often were. Corollary for the eighties: no one can decide that someone else should become a martyr.

7. You are called upon to be who you are where you are, not to be somebody else somewhere else. Dan Berrigan and Bill Coffin and Jane Fonda are signs but not necessarily models. Inadmissible attitude: everybody to the left of me is rash, everybody to the right of me is chicken.

Ideologically, however, you had better be somewhere else tomorrow than where you are today.

8. The maintenance of credibility is difficult but worth struggling for. It can also be a cop-out. If you want to be heard by the middle class, wear a tie, or at least a turtleneck, and keep your hair cut. Do not give people the chance to dismiss you for the wrong reasons. But in making such concessions, remember that you will be tempted so to temper your habits and speech that no offense will be given to the people you want to reach.

9. A variant on #8: cultivate wall-eyed vision. Keep one eye firmly fixed on tomorrow, the other on the long future.

Variant on the variant: Don't wait until all the facts are in before you act. The facts are never all in.

10. The worst things our government does in foreign policy are not deviations from an otherwise good policy; they are only examples of a bad policy. Handy shorthand version of that policy: "If we can do it without bombs we will, but if we cannot, then bombs will do." Therefore:

11. Learn to distrust almost everything a public official says, even about motherhood. Those who struggled in the sixties could all wear buttons with the letters "DBW" (Disillusioned Before Watergate). Johnson and Nixon consistently lied to us. So, probably, did JFK. Carter sounds more and more like them all. The White House will house no savior.

12. Corollary of #11: don't trust the "experts"; they usually disagree among themselves. A great moment of truth in the sixties: the initial hearings of the Fulbright Committee after the Gulf of Tonkin incident, when the Southeast Asia "experts" called in by the Committee turned out to have a totally different reading than the Southeast Asia "experts" called in by the White House. Always try to figure out to whom the "experts" are beholden, especially on such new issues as nuclear energy or arms escalation.

13. A further corollary of #11: be more willing to trust the young. In the sixties they even radicalized their parents.

Translation for the eighties: *be more willing to trust the hurting*. Minorities, women, and the unemployed have a stake in a better world for all. They might even radicalize us.

14. A pair of paradoxes. First paradox: don't overestimate victories, but don't underestimate them either. Second paradox: don't underestimate defeats, but don't overestimate them either. Even the victories may be instances of co-optation; a battle won in the courts may only have been possible because you were from the middle class; a black or a Chicano might have lost.

But cherish the victories. Never agree that the sixties went down the drain, or that the protest was for naught. Public sentiment did turn against the war. Millions were conscienticized. A thousand will never be the same again.

The system appears to have survived basically unscathed through the seventies. But it only appears so. It is creaking. It cannot stem inflation. It cannot cope with minority needs. It cannot risk putting the resources into harnessing the sun that it put into getting a man on the moon. It cannot tolerate full employment. Things will clearly get a lot worse before they can get any better. Precisely the definition of a revolutionary situation . . .

15. Don't try to reanimate the old issues. No need to worry, new issues will come along. By the late seventies, the battlefronts were shifting to the need to reverse the arms race in opposition to those sloganeering under the banner of "national security," to issue some heavy challenges to the proponents of nuclear energy, to support new groups of oppressed peoples, such as homosexuals, in their struggle to live with dignity in a society becoming more and more oppressive.

Note well: the new issues will probably put you in opposition to the same old crowd that brought you Vietnam and napalm.

16. Don't try to go it alone. You will begin to believe the things they are saying about you. You will also become a candidate for early burnout. To have some kind of community is an absolute necessity. A community in the here and now is important; a community with linkages to the past is equally so. To press the point all the way, you need to recognize that your final accountability is not even to your community but only to God. Personal confession: the thing that got me through the sixties and seventies was Luther's hymn, *"A Mighty Fortress Is Our God"*!

> And though this world with devils filled,
> Should threaten to undo us,
> We will not fear, for God hath willed
> [God's] truth to triumph through us:

> Let goods and kindred go,
> This mortal life also;
> The body they may kill;
> God's truth abideth still;
> [God's] kingdom is forever.

It looks like I'll need it in the eighties, too.

PART TWO:

Movements of Grace

To speak of grace is to say that the things most worth expecting are the things that are unexpected. Our explicit anticipations will be fulfilled or disappointed. But those things we do not anticipate, those things that come as surprise—ah, those are the moments that reshape us and nurture us for yet more surprises.

Sometimes grace comes as *admonition*. We make a patently wrong decision and have to pay a price, or we invest too much trust in a person or cause and are disappointed, even burned. Or there is great loss . . . how can we call that grace? There is a line beyond which I, at least, cannot. I will not call the death of a child anything but evil. I will not call collective evil, whether holocaust or war, a sign from God. But there are *some* dislocations through which, while grace may initially be a stern teacher, it is finally a healing presence. In the sixties, Sydney made a silk screen of the first line of Cowper's hymn:

> Ye fearful saints, fresh courage take;
> The clouds ye so much dread

> Are big with mercy, and shall break
> In blessings on your head.

Line one I need every day. Lines two, three, and four I buy, but
only up to a point. I repeat: I will never say that the clouds
above Auschwitz were "big with mercy," or that the clouds
surrounding a dead child have broken open "in blessings." But
granting certain perimeters beyond which the point cannot be
pressed save in diabolical ways, I look within those perimeters for
healing and new strength. I will try to affirm such moments as at
least occasions for graceful response: how can we so use evil that
good may finally come?

But it is the times of *creative surprise* that are the real pointers
to grace:

a stranger walks into one's life and a friendship abides;

a chance encounter is the initiation of a series of planned
encounters and a marriage of thirty-six years' duration results;

a piece of music is first heard by the chance spinning of a
radio dial or a randomly selected phonograph record or because
someone happened to play that piece and not another—and it
becomes an instrument of healing in subsequent times of spiritual fever.

To speak of grace is to say that finally our lives are not our
own, that we are not only recipients of a gift we did not create,
the very gift of life itself, but that throughout our life we are
given gifts we do not deserve—friends, experiences, joy in the
midst of pain—and that at the end we will be upheld by a power
we do not control, promising a fulfillment not of what we have
crafted, but of what the giver of grace continually crafts through
us, with us, and despite us.

Yes, we are those who craft our lives.

Yes, we are even more those whose lives are crafted.

The best moments are those when we perceive, in however
dim a way, that our own intentionalities are working, not at cross
purposes with, but in some kind of harmony with, the divine
intentionality that wills good and not evil, and seeks, working
through the freedom that is indubitably ours, for the fulfillment
of our grace-filled lives.

It is grace that makes the dislocations creative rather than destructive. It invests the dislocations with new possibilities, puts them in a broader framework, offers us a perspective from which God can sometimes turn to good what others may have meant for ill.

A final word is necessary. Grace is a wide word, available to all. Grace is also a narrow word, appropriated by Christians to describe "the grace of our Lord Jesus Christ." It is a way of pointing to the freely given gift of God's presence in our midst in Jesus of Nazareth, whose life was so fully human, so totally an enactment of the divine agenda for all persons, that we affirm the divine as having been present in him in a unique way. This sharing, giving love—which we do not deserve but which is continually offered to us despite our undeserving—reaches a culmination in Jesus' death, victim of a Roman mania for law and order that could not abide the intrusion of unmerited love onto the human scene. And in the playing out of the drama between God's love and human stubbornness, it is God's love that finally conquers. So much and more the resurrection story tells us.

I try to order my life as a response to that claim. By many of my friends the claim is rejected—quickly, angrily, or wistfully. And while I affirm it in theory with the words of my mouth or the keys of my typewriter, I reject it in fact with the feeble quality of my response. But it is at least the center around which I orbit and toward which I try to gravitate. It validates me. I do not validate it.

It is in the light of that sort of grace that I seek to make my dislocations creative, or, more properly, let them be made creative for me.

8

Annunciation
Is Harder Than Denunciation:

On the Other Hand . . .

Yes, annunciation is harder than denunciation. It is harder to announce and provide a creative alternative to something we don't like (whether it is fascism, the current standing of the Boston Red Sox, or certain forms of church music) than it is to denounce and lambaste something we don't like (whether, just to keep the symmetry, it is fascism, the current standing of the Boston Red Sox, or certain forms of church music).

On the other hand . . . denunciation is not all that easy either. For denunciation frequently involves being critical of ideas or institutions that have been beneficial to us, and such criticism often sounds like ingratitude, particularly if we are simultaneously accepting gifts and slapping the hands of the donor. And there is a further problem (for me, at least, a very painful one) that denunciation often involves strong challenges to the convictions of close friends, many of whom are deeply devoted to things in which I no longer believe. Not to put too fine a point on it, relationships are strained. But real friendships can survive such threats. I hope they survive the next few pages.

My problem is very simple, and consequently very difficult: a major impact of the sixties and seventies on me is that I no longer believe in the system that has sustained and supported me, and that is still believed in by the great majority of the people with whom I spend my life. The system has been good to me. It is a major dislocation that I can no longer rest comfortably within it.

The system—capitalism, free enterprise, "the American way of life," a free market economy, whatever term is used—is beneficent in the ears of some, menacing in the ears of others. The terms of such differentiation are easily arrived at: it is beneficent to those who benefit from it, menacing to those who are macerated by it. To most readers of this book it is the former; to many (I believe most) inhabitants of the rest of the world it is the latter.

The reasons for this seemingly harsh judgment began to surface in an earlier section, "Look Out, Your Globe Is Shrinking." The perception of North Americans is that the more we extend our way of life to the rest of the world, the better it will be for the rest of the world, and (not-so-incidentally) for us as well. But the perception of much of the rest of the world is that our businesses, our foreign policy, our military presence, work almost exclusively to our advantage and to their disadvantage. The net result is that we, who were already rich, get richer, and they, who were already poor, get poorer.

This is the overwhelming testimony of those Christians from the Third-World to whom I have had to listen with increasing seriousness over the last ten years: the system that benefits us destroys them.

Note well: I am *not* saying that the people who run our corporations, devise our foreign policy, and supervise our military might, are looking for ways to exploit the poor, see to it that children starve, and ensure that family life in Third-World countries is destroyed. I *am* saying that with the best of intentions to provide other consequences than those, the end result of what well-intentioned people are doing today is frequently exploitation, starvation, and destruction. And I am increasingly led to wonder how it could be otherwise with a system that is built on competition as a way of life (which means that the optimal situation is the elimination of your competitor), and which puts financial profit at the top of the scale of values, considerably above persons.

There's another side to it as well: the system also threatens to destroy its beneficiaries as well as its victims. More and more we are discovering that not all that many corporation executives who have Made It Big have happy family lives, for example. (Ask their wives. Better still, ask them.) They might wish it were different, but, as they will be the first to say, they are "locked in" to the system. It is too late to change their way of life. There are too many mortgage payments pending, too many career expectations forced on them by others, too much fear that overt criticism of the system will mean being passed over if not "terminated," too much manipulation into wind-up people who perform on demand, taking survival cues from someone else rather than expressing who they really are. (A friend of mine, clerking in a chain store, saw a painter begin to lose his balance on top of a ladder. The store manager, observing the incipient accident, and with nary a thought for the poor painter, immediately commented to my friend, "If he spills any paint on my merchandise, I'll break his damn neck!" My friend, still refers to the episode as his Conversion Experience.)

Advocates of the system teach us not to worry about the far-reaching consequences of our corporate deeds (the negative impact of our business on Brazil's poor, for example) so long as the immediate consequences (bigger profits for the stockholders back home) are lucrative. They assuage our moral concerns by telling us that good things for us will trickle down into good things for the others.

I no longer believe it. I am overwhelmed by the evidence that what happens is that the gap between rich and poor increases. Denunciation is not so hard . . . .

But if denunciation is not so hard, annunciation of an alternative is not so easy. In fact, it is very hard. I don't know how to do it yet, and I'm not sure I ever will. I'm not even fully convinced that it is my job to do it. But it certainly is the task of Christians to demand and explore alternatives and to insist that no fear or smear tactics be used to shut off exploration of alternatives prematurely. (The recoil with which the word *socialism* is heard in even the most enlightened church circles today is only a tiny symbol of how un-free we are when it comes to looking at our world.) And it is certainly the task of Christians to make it possible for all people to affirm and live out alternatives and options that appeal to them. Only in the experimentation of living out alternatives can we discover whether one or a number of them will work.

I see three possible kinds of annunciation possible in the United States today. I am afraid the first is irrelevant and that the second is unlikely. I hope the third is important.

1. The irrelevant option is the liberal option briefly explored a little earlier in this book. It involves constant attempts at cosmetic improvement of the present system, tinkering around the edges so that some of the grossest inequities are overcome. That is surely better than nothing—particularly for those who are victims of the grossest inequities—and might survive if the inequities were merely gross. But it seems to me irrelevant for two reasons: first, it does not really change anything since it fails to go to the root of the problem which is the evil inherent in the system itself; and second, it can deceive us into thinking

that because we have done a little tinkering we have done enough and can rest complacently within the system that continues to perpetuate the inequities.

2. The unlikely option is the so-called revolutionary one, but even before I complete the sentence I have to add two qualifications: (a) what may be unlikely in the United States right now may be likely elsewhere, and (b) the modifier "so-called" is crucial. I am convinced that Christians are called upon to be revolutionaries—the gospel will allow for nothing else—but I am also convinced that there are revolutionaries and revolutionaries. A popular view of revolution in the activist sixties, for example, assumed that we could easily transport Third-World models of violent revolution to the United States, since "the masses" were ripe for action and were only waiting for a charismatic leader. To recall such a position today may seem to be an instance of flailing a dead horse, but there are still people who are so distressed and outraged by the present order of things that they believe one big strong *push* might topple the whole system; it happened twenty years ago in Cuba, it happened recently in Nicaragua and it could happen elsewhere by the time this appears in print. Why couldn't it happen here?

It's an attractive theory to those who feel that radical change is long overdue, but does it really speak to the North American situation?

Going against it is the claim that we are hardly in a "pre-revolutionary situation." Despite growing fears about inflation and energy and jobs, there are still too many people who "never had it so good," and who will stick with the known rather than risk the unknown. Even if they don't "have it so good" right now, their welfare payments or unemployment insurance are just sufficient to defuse their revolutionary fervor or just precarious enough to cause them to fear that "making trouble" might dry up the benefits. In addition, there are other people (and they happen to possess massive power) who have such a vested interest in the status quo that they are quite ready to put all that power to work defending it—economic, political, *and military*. Those who believe that change is desperately needed had better believe also that change will be desperately resisted.

On the other side of the ledger, however, are two facts I now take more seriously than I did even a few months ago.

First and longer fact: we may be closer to a "pre-revolutionary situation" than we think. Those "growing fears about inflation and energy and jobs" (to take only a sampling of concerns close at hand) are real, and they breed protest. Protest in the sixties was nurtured mainly out of concern for others (particularly blacks and Vietnamese). Protest in the eighties will retain that concern but it will be more powerful, for it will be augmented by concern for self. Not only other people's jobs but *my* job may be on the line; not only will people in cold climates be cold next winter because of the price of oil, but *I* probably will be also. If my interests alone were at stake, fascism would be an attractive option. But in the eighties—in a way that was not true in the sixties—*everybody's* interests are at stake, and their survival is far from certain. Maybe the system can't deliver this time. And if we go down the tube, most of us (or at least a lot of us) will be in on the ride, like it or not.

Now when concern for self and concern for others begin to coincide, powerful forces are being unleashed. And, to take only one example, the chinks in the armor of corporations plugging atomic energy are beginning to show. They are vulnerable when confronting "the power of the people," and the people are beginning to find that out.

Second and shorter fact: the "one big strong *push*" that sounds so easy to the romantics, doesn't happen overnight. Decades of preparation work precede it; after all, it was forty years before the Somoza regime was toppled. *But more preparatory work has gone on than we realize.* Surely that is part of what the sixties and seventies were all about. Maybe the truly "revolutionary" posture today will be to continue long-range, patient, sometimes unromantic efforts to raise the level of consciousness about just how the system works and what are the realistic possibilities of its replacement.

That kind of revolution isn't so unlikely.

3. All of which points toward the third option, the form of annunciation that could be important, rather than irrelevant or unlikely. It involves not only thinking about alternatives but trying to create some right now. It means recognizing that Exxon, Gulf and Western, the State Department, and the Pentagon are neither going to be converted into beneficent sharers of the world's resources with the world's poor, nor are they going to fold their tents and quietly steal away. The needed annunciation will not be so much a frontal attack on them, as a decision to offer people some parallel structures through which they can try, on a variety of scales of magnitude, to demonstrate that life can be lived cooperatively rather than competitively, that people can count for more than profits, and that the growing gap between the rich and poor can at least begin to be reversed if not eliminated. The attempt to create countermodels would be a way of saying, "Let us try to demonstrate in the *present* what we would like the world to be in the *future*."

Such an annunciation could be the conscienticizing tool toward a revolution twenty-five years from now, either violent or nonviolent. But if it caught on at all, it would render the violent revolution unnecessary. For a quiet but more thorough revolution would have occurred along the way.

I want to explore the tentative beginnings of this form of annunciation later on. But before doing so, I want to extend the denunciation/annunciation theme in another direction: what would it mean to talk about denunciation and annunciation in relation to God?

9

On Denouncing God:

(Denouncing God? . . .)

Not only must we be able to express our anger at the system, the world, and all the evil we find surrounding us, we must also be able to express that anger toward God. It is part of the life of faith to be able to rebel, to quarrel, to get mad at God.

The notion will strike many Christians as blasphemous. Who are *we* to challenge the ways of the Almighty? What pretension!

But perhaps it is more than pretension. Perhaps it is a sign of how much we care, that we dare to express our outrage even toward the One who created us. This is a lesson Christians need to learn from Jews, who have a long history of questioning the ways of God—and not at all surprising, since of all God's creatures, Jews are the ones with most reason to question both God's love and God's justice. (My sister, pained by a tragedy in her own life, said in more than half-jest to a Jewish friend, "If I ever make it to heaven, I'm going to line up at the throne of God and ask, 'Why did you arrange it so that things like this could happen?' " "Hattie," was his instantaneous response, "it's a very long line . . .")

In the face of so much evil, denunciation should be a part of being truly human. We should occasionally be emboldened to shout (or scream) in the midst of our pain or the pain of another, "A universe like this, who needs it? If this is an example of your love, thanks but no thanks."

Perhaps only after we can be that honest in our denunciation is there a possibility for annunciation to be reborn. In *The Town Beyond the Wall* (Avon Books, 1964), Elie Wiesel, who has had more reason than most of us to denounce, places on the lips of one of his most rebellious characters the despairing and yet strangely hopeful words:

> I want to blaspheme, and I can't quite manage it. I go up against [God], I shake my fist, I froth with rage, but it's still a way of telling Him that He's there, that He exists, that He's never the same twice, that denial itself is an offering to His grandeur. The shout becomes a prayer in spite of me. (p. 123)

That we care enough to be angry is important. For *caring is a key that opens many doors*. The supreme insult we can pay to another human being is to behave as though that person did not exist, to refuse any response, even to indignity. *Any* response is better than no response, since it is at least an acknowledgment that the other matters enough to elicit a response, even though the response may be one of anger or hurt. So, analogously, it is not a matter of impiety to be angry with God; it is an acknowledgment that God matters to us.

Once we get over that initial hurdle, we may then be able to move beyond denunciation toward annunciation, from negation toward affirmation. If the denunciation is hard, the annunciation will probably be even harder. But it might get closer to the true nature of reality.

To turn to Wiesel again (who has been my preeminent instructor in these matters), he once followed Richard Rubenstein on a program in which Rubenstein, with great poignancy, lamented how difficult it was to live in a world without God, a world in which God had been destroyed by the events of the holocaust. Wiesel put aside his prepared script and spoke directly to Rubenstein's concern, pointing out that if it is hard to live a life of negation, it is even harder to live a life of affirmation. "If you want difficulties," he said, "choose to live *with* God. Can you compare the tragedy of the believer to that of the nonbeliever? The real tragedy, the real drama, is the drama of the believer."

That may initially seem a strange form of affirmation. But it is an honest and unblinking one. It beats cheap annunciation. It appears only on the far side of denunciation. But the terrain on which it is located is the terrain of faith.

10

Beyond the Guilt Trip Trap

"Being a Presbyterian," I was once told and have frequently verified, "doesn't keep you from sinning, but it sure keeps you from enjoying it." The cumulative impact of these pages may well seem like a cunning Presbyterian trick to pile up unrelieved anxiety, in order to make people, especially people like myself (white, male, middle-class, bourgeois, still tinged with chauvinism), feel as guilty as possible. Michael Novak, a Catholic friend, once tried to explain my penchant for criticizing my country and my class, by saying to another Catholic, "You just don't understand. Protestants *like* to feel guilty. It makes them feel good."

It may look that way, but it doesn't really feel that way. Martin Buber has made a helpful distinction between guilt and guilt feelings. Guilt feelings can be dealt with psychiatrically or therapeutically or with plain commonsense; we discover that our feelings of guilt are misplaced, morbid, or masochistic. But to the degree that we are in fact guilty (which I insist we sometimes are) there is no rationalization to persuade us that it isn't so. If we *are* guilty, the only release is grace, grace as forgiveness. And since I believe in forgiveness, I don't have to scurry around to escape a provisional verdict of guilty, since the final divine stamp upon the one who acknowledges wrongdoing is not "sinner" but "forgiven sinner." This is not to presume on forgiveness by sinning bravely that grace may abound (as a character in Auden's *For the Time Being* put it, "I like committing sins, God likes forgiving them. Really, the world is admirably arranged"), but it is to say that the final word is never guilt and therefore despair, but always forgiveness and therefore hope. So guilt is a *provisional* estimate of who we are; we can acknowledge it with utmost seriousness when we realize that it is not a *final* estimate of who we are.

Having said that much for guilt, let us go on to note that guilt is never a good motivation for action, particularly action on behalf of others. A certain kind of theology pushes guilt very hard, assuming that if we can really be persuaded of our guilt, a guilt induced by our own self-centeredness, we will rise to herculean efforts to "make up for it" by selfless actions on behalf of others. It may sometimes be the case that we do rise to herculean efforts, but if we do it out of guilt or in order to overcome guilt, we are not finally doing it "on behalf of others," but on behalf of ourselves. We are trying to wipe the slate clean, or make ourselves feel better, or even up the score on the Great Ledger that worried Steinbeck's Doc—a character we will encounter later on. Such actions are motivated by a high level of self-concern and a low level of other-directed concern. The other becomes someone we "use" for our own cleansing, rather than someone to whom the fullness of our being is directed.

A friend recently described me as "greedy for purity." It wasn't meant as a compliment, though if Kierkegaard is right that "purity of heart is to will one thing," a fixation on

purity might just be the first step toward sanctity. I won't try
to avoid the indictment, however, by the route of incipient
sainthood. What the friend meant, I believe, was that
certain people, of whom I was a chief exemplar, want at any
cost to be free of guilt, to be "pure," and that as a result they
live rather unrealistic lives. To him, my increasing
restlessness at Stanford because I was going in different
directions than it was, and my belief that Union's direction
was too "centrist" for me to work happily within it, were
instances of opting out of corporate responsibility in order
to insure individual purity.

It's a healthy, if not particularly flattering, reminder of a
temptation all of us have to face, which is to seek personal
purity at the cost of concern for others. We would like to opt
out of "compromising" situations, disengage from structures that do not fully please us, and find one little island of
uncontaminated goodness, possibly inhabited by a few
people very much like ourselves.

I have news for all of us: there is no longer any such place.
The last one was named Eden, and the ease with which it
was invaded by less than the purest motives should be a
reminder that no place, structure, group, or situation will
be other than an example of a fallen creation. There is no
"guiltless place."

But let us turn the argument around: those who are
suspicious of people "greedy for purity" need to wrestle
with their own particular temptation, which is to settle too
comfortably into "compromising" situations, and become
content with token opposition that is always sliding toward
total capitulation. In such cases it becomes increasingly easy
to let our goals be determined by what is "practical" or
"reasonable" or "achievable." The spoiler is that *someone else*
defines the actions that correspond to such goals. I know;
I've walked that road many times. It represents not so much
an act of ill will as a failure of the imagination. Who knows
what could actually be done, until we move beyond low-

level estimates of what is "possible"? In this arena, a little more "greed" might benefit us all.

The problem, then, is to determine where to draw the line between staying in and getting out. The solution, naturally, will involve different people drawing lines at different places. When I was wrestling with the problem of how I could in conscience participate in World War II, I was greatly helped by a sermon of Reinhold Niebuhr, in which he pointed out that there are various roles Christians can play in society—we can be *prophets* (those who engage in critical judgment against), *priests* (those who work within), or *martyrs* (those who refuse at whatever cost to be beholden). We are not all cast in the same mold, nor are we going to play the same role on every occasion. I discovered that as far as World War II was concerned, my question was not finally, How could I in conscience participate? but, How could I in conscience *not* participate? And yet when it came to the Vietnamese War, the scales of moral judgment were tilted in exactly the opposite direction.

As the earlier chronicle indicates, I have been shifting from a relatively uncritical participation in structures to a much more disenchanted role. This may be partly a function of getting older: I don't want to spend all my time fighting battles to move an institution one inch ahead (or keep it from moving six inches behind) when the task is clearly for everybody to move six inches ahead, or even a foot. It may be less a matter of guilt than of impatience. And it may mean that if the old structures remain unyielding, our task will be to create new ones.

. . . Which is what I want to explore in the next section. But there is a transition first, a transition dealing with the *motivation* by which we not only escape from the guilt trip trap but move from it back into the world of social responsibility.

How much do we let what we *want* to do with our lives determine what we actually do? There was a strong streak in my upbringing that militated against even asking the question. Duty, obligation, surrender of my will to God's will (which almost always seemed to be the polar opposite of mine)—*these* were the touchstones of Christian decision-making. (One thing that delayed my decision to go to Stanford in 1962 was a residual Calvinist feeling that it must be wrong to move from grim New York to pleasant California; only the morally flabby would do such a thing.)

I no longer believe we can slug out a lifetime of Christian witness by placing our total offering on an altar marked "obligation." There has got to be a measure of *joy* in what we do, an anticipation of excitement when we face the day, rather than a dull feeling of boredom or resentment at what lies ahead. Some may call this "selfish" (Calvinists immediately begin to cover their tracks), but I am surer and surer that unless there *is* joy in what we do, the results will not only be drab and cheerless for us but also for those with whom we work.

Coupled with my misgivings about remaining at Union this last time around was a sense that I ought to stay on anyhow, out of a sense of obligation (to what, never came quite clear). But that motivation would never have been enough to engender the enthusiasm needed for the job. It would have been a recipe for disaster. I realized that it was important to wake up without a lead weight attached to my spirit; to face the day as stretching ahead with freeing possibilities rather than limiting constrictions; to face the joy of scaling down to the actual possibilities of twelve brief hours, rather than the necessity of revving up to the grim realities of twelve endless hours.

Is that indulgent? We'll see—not so much in whether I gain a liberated spirit, but in whether or not, with a liberated spirit, I can share that liberation with a measure of ecstasy, a quality my friends have not previously been inclined to attach to my name.

11

Maybe "Small Is Beautiful" But Bigness Isn't Going Away

If small *is* beautiful, then a small section on that topic should bring aesthetic pleasure to the reader. Let me see if I can oblige.

I discovered in the sixties that large structures could be perverse. I want to be less beholden to them so that they do not set all my agendas. But I also discovered in the seventies that large structures can be timid. And I want to be less beholden on that score also, for I sometimes have the feeling that timidity is the most subtle of all temptations. ("Better something doubtful or overbold, and therefore in need of forgiveness," Karl Barth wrote in one of his most inspired moments, "than nothing at all. . . .")

If large structures are counterproductive of good ends, perhaps smaller structures could be instruments of creativity. That used to strike me as "naïve" and "romantic" (two favorite pejoratives of my earlier theological life). I knew then, and know even better now, that evil is present, not only in human hearts, but also in human structures; and in recent years have observed that in those structures it can acquire an almost independent power of its own, so that good individuals with the best of intentions can be party to great corporate evil. Indeed, the larger the structure, the greater the ease with which this can happen, and the greater the ease with which an individual in such a structure can get off the hook of moral accountability for what the structure does.

In the face of that, there is, I am coming to believe, a chance in smaller structures to retain some sense of moral accountability and to turn such structures toward creative rather than destructive ends. This doesn't just mean creating small businesses, for example, where persons can be treated as persons, group decision-making is possible, and a humane atmosphere can be maintained. It also means finding ways within the large structures to establish small centers of work-sharing where, likewise, persons can be treated as persons, group decision-making with account-ability is possible, and a human atmosphere can be maintained. This is not just dreamy nonsense. It is already beginning to happen within corporations, government agencies, and educational institutions. It could even happen within seminaries. (A highly placed executive in the automotive industry, challenged by Sydney to consider such an approach in his plants, responded immediately that it wouldn't. work. Too impractical. "But," he reflected immediately thereafter, "it might cut down the on-the-job sabotage.")

So, *on the one hand*, I am increasingly persuaded that Schumacher is right and that (as the title of his book puts it) *Small Is Beautiful* (Harper & Row, 1973). In the best of all possible worlds, we could turn our backs on destructive bigness and commit ourselves to creative smallness—small creative workplaces, small creative communities, small creative political parties, small creative collectives for economic interdependence.

We can't. It's not the best of all possible worlds. There is always an *on the other hand*. In this case, the counterpart to "small is beautiful" is that "bigness isn't going away." We have to take account of that, too.

Big political structures are a case in point. If we choose, as was proposed above, to "turn our backs" on large scale politics, that abdication glosses over a moral failure we cannot ignore, namely that such abdication is not abdication at all, but a vote by default for whoever has power. Not to take sides is to take sides. The spectator, Elie Wiesel reminds us, ends up supporting executioners rather than victims. Example: during the 1968 presidential campaign I was hard put to support Hubert Humphrey because of his aggressive advocacy of our Vietnam policy. I mentioned this to Andy Young, out at Stanford to preach one Sunday. He replied, kindly but tellingly, "That's a privilege white liberals have that we blacks don't have. If we don't vote for Humphrey, Nixon will win, and he'll appoint federal judges in the southern courts who will set civil rights back a hundred years." I supported Humphrey.

There is another reason to continue working within the big structures, and Andy Young's comment points in its direction also: it is a fact that even if big structures do not accomplish much clear good, they can sometimes prevent clear harm. "The law may not be able to make the white man love me," Martin Luther King, Jr., used to say, "but it can keep the white man from lynching me, and I think that's pretty important."

So do I. It is a compelling reason to continue to work within the big structures: *they can hold back some evil, even if they cannot advance much good*. A relatively cheerful conclusion to salvage out of two distressing decades.

But not yet a good enough conclusion for a section already threatening to lose its aesthetic component by becoming too long. So herewith are three swift conclusions about smallness and bigness:

1. Since small is beautiful, let us develop new areas in our lives where it can be operative—at work, among friends, through support groups.

2. Since bigness isn't going away, let us view small structures not merely as islands of sanity in a cruel world, but as ongoing alternative possibilities that can offer challenges to, or be components of, the big structures. To the degree that they accomplish what used to be accomplished only in the centers of large corporate power, their attractiveness will grow. (Theological footnote: This, I discover, is a slightly revised version of the old Catholic "principle of subsidiarity": let decision-making powers be as widely diffused as possible and let no higher group assume powers that can be exercised by a lower group—save that the implied hierarchical principle is also being challenged.)

3. Since small is beautiful but bigness isn't going away, let us keep one foot (never more than one foot) in the big structures, seeking to be a leaven in them, and, in canny fashion, using them in ways they may not intend. (I offer a tentative example in the postscript.)

The goal of such concerns is to strengthen an already existing network into a movement sufficiently strong to challenge present power structures—locally at first, but on regional and national levels as well. It includes energy collectives, antinuclear coalitions, minority groups, the elderly, women's collectives, small businesses, church groups, experimental educational ventures—all those folk who have previously thought that they were powerless but are beginning to realize that they needn't stay that way.

Such strengthening is already going on. It is not being ignored by those whose power it threatens. We can look for new attempts at preferential legislation on behalf of those who now hold power (development of solar energy will be a good case study), accompanied by more and more folksy ads from the Mobil people, telling us to put our trust in them, since all the alternatives are unrealistic.

I think they're already too late.

Postscript:

On Working Within Caesar's Household Without Becoming Caesar's Slave: A Fantasy on Theological Education

For those to whom the above material seems to represent the generalized comments of a nonexpert, I offer one specific scenario in the field of seminary education. If it makes any sense there, it could be adapted elsewhere.

Large institutions (such as seminaries) are not likely to be on the forefront of radical social change. Christians are supposed to be on the forefront of radical social change. To bring about radical social change, institutions are both useful and necessary.

Where does one go with that, if one believes that theological education should be a vehicle for radical social change?

I still believe there is *a remnant within the churches* that would respond to the cries of Third-World Christians and examine what changes in life-style, theological methodology, "revisionist" understanding of church history, and so forth, would be called for in preparing to nurture that remnant community.

I used to believe there might be some seminaries where that could happen. I am no longer so sanguine about that. "Established" seminaries are beholden to sources of financial support that would never encourage such a use of funds, and they are dug into institutional histories that make radical change unlikely.

So what is one to do?

One can keep batting one's head against the wall, remaining "the lone voice," the creative minority opinion, tolerated only because not powerful enough to be a significant threat. The price of doing so is constant frustration.

One can adopt a low profile, trying quietly but persistently in one's own teaching and writing to intrude new ideas into structures that want very few of them. The price of doing so is the danger of co-optation.

One can throw in the towel. The price of doing so is likely to be one's soul.

One can start a new seminary, made up of the like-minded. It would not be hard to assemble faculty, but it would be exceedingly difficult to pay them. Other financial needs are (a) a good (i.e., expensive) library, (b) buildings to house library, students, classrooms, faculty and administration, (c) scholarships, since students coming to such a seminary would not be affluent, (d) considerable endowment, once the original donors discovered what was going on and withdrew their support. The price of doing so is out of sight.

(Qualifying note: New York Theological Seminary, courageous enough to break all the rules, solved many of its problems by getting rid of its library, buildings, tenured faculty, and so forth, in a bold venture paralleling some of the concerns described below.)

The above scenarios are inadequate. Could there be another scenario? (Here is where the fantasy comes in.)

Imagine a center of theological learning. It has buildings, library, faculty, endowment, and students, along with a tradition of being open to a few new ideas. What could be done in such a situation to educate the remnant for the future? Some do-it-yourself hints:

a. Accept being part of such a situation. It has a legitimate claim on a portion of one's time and energy.

b. But insist on being *more* than just a "part of such a situation." Alongside the institutional vision set another, alternative vision. Being "in yet not of" an existing structure is part of the Christian legacy. How (in a creative rather than destructive use of the word) could one "exploit" such an institutional structure for ends it may not envision?

c. Possible model: "Seminsem," or, a seminary-within-a-seminary. To be part of Seminsem would mean to be part of a self-conscious intentional community within the overall seminary, as well as part of the overall seminary itself. Dual citizenship. Another part of the Christian legacy. How would it work?

d. Perhaps 75 percent of Seminsem's curriculum could be provided by already existing courses in Bible, church history, systematic theology, ethics. Restlessness about just *how* this material is "provided" necessitates the next provision.

e. At least 25 percent of the curriculum would need to be created by members of Seminsem, both "faculty" and "students" (a distinction of limited value in Seminsem). This would involve asking what one *does,* in an unjust world, with the biblical or historical or ethical material one has acquired, a question conventional seminary courses seem unwilling to face. Another task would be to ask *how* education takes place, i.e., what is deficient in conventional models (thus making Seminsem necessary) and how remedial work can be done before the conventional models destroy one's ability to learn. (Paulo Freire would loom large in such encounters.) There would also be seminars in substantive subject matter, pursued along nontraditional lines—not a case of having an "expert" impart information, but of the initiation of a cooperative exploration of what Christian faith means today.

f. Seminsem would anchor its own life in the community around it—not the "academic" community, but the community of workers, unemployed, artists, politicians, lay church members. The model: theological questions posed *out of* such encounters rather than theological answers imposed *upon* them. Nonseminarians should be present to challenge abstract theorizing. Theological reflection would mature out of commitment to the victims of our society.

g. Seminsem would need a physical center. It might be a house "in town," or a room within the seminary, set apart for Seminsem activities, where those with similar concerns could share insights, frustrations, breakthroughs, hopes, bread and wine.

h. There would be a minimal corporate discipline. The adjectives are important. At the start it should be *minimal,* not making demands that would scare away potential involvement, and the scale of subsequent demands should grow out of the group. And it should be *corporate,* a commitment agreed upon by all and not left to individual whimsy, to share work, study, results, liturgy, chores.

i. Exclusiveness and preciousness would be avoided. All who wish to participate would be welcome.

Seminsem would not be a covert operation. The institution where it is located would be informed of its goals and activity, and its cooperation solicited. Members of Seminsem would create a statement of intention on the basis of which to request space and other amenities from the seminary, seek course credit for Seminsem seminars, and live as an arm of the seminary itself. Although the idea is to subvert inadequate present models, seminary administrators frightened by experimentation should be asked to adopt the Gamaliel test (Acts 5:38): "If this plan or this undertaking is of people alone, it will fail; but if it is of God, you will not be able to overthrow them"—a no-lose situation for any sensitive administrator.

Finally, let all be provisional. Mistakes will be made; they should be acknowleged and rectified. Critique from outside should be sought; critique from inside should be mandatory. The goal is not to create an autonomous institution, but so to transform the existing institution that the need for Seminsem will disappear.

12

The Gift
of Disturbing Discoveries

The *gift* of disturbing discoveries? Who looks upon disturbance as a gift? Not many of us. But if we have spent our lives seeing things one way, and it gets harder and harder to make sense of what we see, then the time has come when we need to be disturbed. And if we then begin to see more clearly, the disturbance has been worthwhile and even deserving of gratitude.

That, at least, has been happening to me. A number of disturbing discoveries have had a revolutionary impact on me. I wouldn't have chosen to have them upset my life. But they have. And I'm beginning to be grateful. Revolutionary grace.

First disturbing discovery: who we listen to determines what we hear.

There's an obvious statement if there ever was one. Of course who we listen to determines what we hear! It is not so obvious, however, that we often take great pains *not* to listen to those who might challenge conclusions to which we have already come. "I've made up my mind," the saying goes, "don't confuse me with the facts."

Martin Buber describes the attitudes of various Germans to Hitler. A few, he concedes, may not have known what was going on. A few did, and acted courageously to oppose Hitler. A lot more did, and became willing accomplices of Hitler's policy. A great many, however, fearing that terrible things were going on, took special pains *not* to find out. They left questions unasked and avoided people who might have answered the unasked questions. They listened only to those who assured them that nothing was amiss, that any tales they had heard were exaggerated, and that anyway whatever was happening to the Jews was for their own good.

The attitude is catching. We, too, choose to whom we will listen. If we wanted to believe that what was going on in Vietnam was good, we listened to the military or to LBJ. If we didn't, we listened to Joan Baez or Abraham Heschel or William Fulbright. What we believed about civil rights was partly determined by whether we listened to George Wallace or Martin Luther King, Jr. What we feel about nuclear energy depends on whether we listen to the energy corporations or the environmentalists. Who we listen to determines what we hear, and we determine to whom we listen.

To whom shall we listen in the eighties? The same ones whom we tried to avoid in the sixties and seventies, but who told us the truth: *the victims.* (Henceforth I will take it as an axiom of Christian living that we must first listen to the victims.) We learned more truth about what was going on in Vietnam from victims of napalm and antipersonnel weapons than we did from Dow Chemical (which made napalm) or Honeywell (which made antipersonnel weapons). Those who could have told the truth about Germany in the thirties were not the Nazis but the Jews. We chose not to listen. When we began to listen, we were six million deaths too late.

So as we try to understand the world of the eighties, we need to listen to the victims, to those who are hurting, whether the Puerto Ricans in New York City, the poor in Latin America, the blacks in South Africa, the political prisoners in South Korea, the gays all over the world, or the increasing number of radiation casualties in our "safe" nuclear power plants.

Second disturbing discovery: where we stand determines what we see.

There's another obvious statement. Of course where we stand determines what we see! If you are on a high sand dune, and I am on the beach a hundred feet below, you can see ships hidden from my eyes. (My wife and I once talked with Andrew McNeal, who has the only croft on Oronsay, a tiny island in the Hebrides. We commented on how beautiful the island was, lamenting only that it was so far away. "From where?" was his laconic response.)

In the sixties, if you were a black, eligible for the draft, you saw the Vietnam War one way; if you were a white, with a college deferment, you saw it another way. In the seventies, if you were one of the designers of the boilers at the Three Mile Island nuclear reactor, you saw the "disaster" there one way; if you were pregnant, living two miles from the power plant, you saw it another way.

Where we stand determines what we see. And where we stand is in itself determined by a lot of things. It has something to do with the color of our skin, the degree of our financial security or insecurity, and whether our last name is Armstrong or Zablocki. It has a lot to do with class. Middle-class white people in America generally see capitalism as a good thing because it has been good to them. Destitute working class Peruvians in "Ciudad de Diós" in Lima have only had oppressive encounters with it. Middle-class white people in America want desperately to believe that all is well, and they believe things that reinforce

their belief that all is well. In the sixties, our presidents were
lying to us, but because their lies reassured us, we accepted
the lies as truth. We accepted the statistics of our Pentagon
officials, even though they were doctoring the statistics like
crazy. In the seventies, we believed our nuclear scientists
when they told us not to worry about "nuclear waste,"
because we all wanted nuclear energy, even though the
scientists had not the slightest idea of how to dispose of
nuclear waste, which we now learn will remain radioactive
for 250,000 years.

Since we won't easily change the place where we are
standing, we will at least have to start by listening to people
who are standing somewhere else and ask them what they
see. It would have made an incalculable difference in the
sixties if we had stood with Martin Luther King, Jr., or even
heard what he saw from where he was standing; if in the
seventies we had stood with the Sandinistas in Nicaragua
instead of with Somoza, and if we had shared the viewpoint
of liberation theologians in Chile rather than executives of
I.T.T. If we continue to stand within a perspective that
concludes that "the United States must remain Number
One at all costs," then we will see only certain things: the
need for more bombers, more napalm, more atomic
weapons; and we will fail to consider the alternatives that
could be paid for out of the funds that will supply those
things, and thereby lose out on new possibilities for our
cities, our minorities, our health, and our environment.
Once again, it is from the standpoint of victims, potential
and actual, that we must try to view the world of the eighties,
if we are to avoid our present collision course with disaster.

Third disturbing discovery:
what we do determines who we are.

That one's not so obvious. But it's equally important. It
represents a wild reversal for me. I used to think it was the

other way around, that who we are determines what we do. But that doesn't work so well for me any more. It implies that there is an easy transition from thought to action: work out a world view, and then "apply it." That becomes a nifty rationalization for the status quo. People say they are for love—and find it possible to build and fly B-52's against defenseless peasants. People say they believe in sacrifice and worry their heads off about their retirement benefit programs. We find it too easy to say who we are, engage in actions that are the exact contrary, and not even be aware that we have a problem.

The opposite route is more accurate. Our self-definitions are not constructed in our heads; they are forged by our deeds. The payoff is not a consistent theory, but a committed life.

A jaw-breaking theological distinction may help. On the one hand there is *orthodoxy*, which means "right belief," and on the other hand there is *orthopraxis*, which means "right action." Orthodoxy is what goes on in our heads, which may or may not get translated into our lives. Orthopraxis is what goes on in our lives, and it lays right out for everybody just who we are. The deed defines the person: "Manuel" is the one who organized the strike of the textile workers, he can be trusted; "Isabel" is the one who organized the hunger strike on behalf of the "disappeareds," she can be trusted too. General Pinochet, on the other hand, says that he believes in God, and General Pinochet encourages the torture of political prisoners; he cannot be trusted. The normative reality about General Pinochet is not professed belief in God, but actual torturing of prisoners. What he does tells us who he is, not the other way around. It is axiomatic for me that no one can torture political prisoners and believe in God. As far as belief in the Christian God is concerned, General Pinochet is an atheist.

The example amplifies the point that *there is no neutrality*. One is either for or against the torture of political prisoners;

one sides with the victim or with the torturer. The sophisticated usually dismiss such an analysis as "simplistic." It is, in fact, simplistic, but not in the way the sophisticated think. It is simplistic to the extent that it omits another possibility: rather than being a victim or a torturer, one can be a spectator, standing on the sidelines, refusing to get involved, saying that the evidence pro and con isn't all in yet (a favorite dodge of the sophisticated and particularly the academically sophisticated). But even that is still too simplistic because in fact spectators are not spectators; they have sided with the torturers, turning over their proxies to others to do the dirty work. The "spectator" is really saying, "You can go ahead and torture, because even though I may not cheer you on, you can bank on the fact that I won't oppose you."

If we prescind from the question of the torture of political prisoners, we are complicit in the torture that is encouraged by our inaction. We may define ourselves as Episcopalians or professors or social analysts, committed to "examining both sides of the question," but to the victims of the torture we will appear as complicit in their suffering. We are not defined by rhetoric but by deeds. What we do determines who we are.

Fourth disturbing discovery:
when we have made three disturbing discoveries,
everything is up for grabs.

Well, almost everything. And even with the slight qualification, a single example can make the point. As I indicated earlier, I am the product of a generation that was educated to see our nation as exerting a beneficent influence on the rest of the world. We aid those in distress, help those in need, share our technology with less fortunate peoples, and generally lend a helping hand. If people don't appreciate our help, they are being ungrateful.

I am now having to entertain a contrary analysis. It haunts and disquiets me, a brooding presence that refuses to go away. I offer it not as a foolproof alternative but as a highly entertainable (not entertaining) alternative. I will state it baldly, for the sake of the contrast.

It is possible to interpret our role in Vietnam (quite contrary to the official rhetoric of "helping" the Vietnamese) as an effort to protect, shore up, and expand our American business interests, our international political prestige, and our overall economic well-being—an example, a particularly brutal example, of how an imperialistic nation tries to dominate a former colonial nation for its own interests, rather than the interests of the Vietnamese.

The analysis gains credence by the fact that there are plenty of examples of our employing the same pattern elsewhere. In 1973—after we could have been expected to have "learned" from Vietnam—we did the same thing to Chile, only in Chile we didn't have to use napalm, B-52s and antipersonnel weapons. We merely financed and supported the coup of the Chilean military junta, and sponsored the installation and maintenance of one of the most brutal governments of modern times. As Henry Kissinger, then secretary of state, commented in a moment of candor, there was no reason to let Chile go communist just because the Chileans didn't know any better.

It was the same mentality we had used toward Vietnam. The difference is that our policy has succeeded (I hope only temporarily) in Chile, whereas it was defeated (I hope permanently) in Vietnam. We duplicated the maneuver in Iran, seeking to back the Shah. We lost there too. We have been trying for twenty years to destroy Cuba by an economic blockade, having failed abysmally in our support of a military invasion at the Bay of Pigs or in numerous assassination attempts against Fidel Castro. Goliath is unable to conquer David.

When I look at such events through the eyes of the victims—the Vietnamese, the Chileans, the Iranians, the Cubans—I see a consistent pattern: in order to thwart the expansion of any socialist (let alone communist) regime, we will do whatever is necessary to achieve that end. If we can do it without bombs or assassinations we will—through convert CIA operations, blockades, attempts to bribe the leaders of the foreign governments, supporting right-wing dissidents within the countries, or whatever. It does not matter whether the citizens of the country have chosen their regime in a free election, as the Chileans did; *we* will decide what is good for *them*. And what is "good" for them is what is good for us, i.e., our own economic and political security. So dictators, no matter how ruthless, can count on our support if they play the game our way.

Talk about disturbances, dislocations . . . To the degree that the above analysis is even partly on target, thirty years of my perceptions are being dissolved in illusion. Bitter-sweet grace.

Such an analysis will probably upset a lot of readers, just as it initially upset me. My response is that the truth tends to upset a lot of things. And while it does not necessarily follow that anything that upsets us is the truth, there is a simple test by which to validate or invalidate the analysis. It goes like this: let us listen to the victims, the hurting, the oppressed, as they tell us how the world looks through their eyes, and especially how the United States looks through their eyes. And then, in the light of what we hear, let us entertain the possibility that if what they tell us is true, a lot of what we have previously believed and taken for granted simply has to be put up for grabs.

That by itself might seem overwhelming and destructive, particularly if much of what we have taken for granted does turn out to be vulnerable. So let us examine a final disturbing discovery, one that can also be liberating.

Fifth disturbing (but also liberating) discovery: where we come from says a lot about where we are going, but it needn't lock us in.

The thing that does lock us in is our unwillingness to reexamine our past assumptions, because it would be too threatening to do so. In that case, we *are* locked in to our pasts: middle-class assumptions we have inherited are not open to reexamination, masculine prejudices must be retained unexamined, white perspectives dare not be compared with nonwhite perspectives. Santayana's famous statement deserves repetition one time more: "Those who ignore history are doomed to repeat it." If we live out of our past conditioning, unaware of what we are doing, then our actions will be predictible to a high degree: we will be for whatever preserves things unchanged and against whatever or whoever proposes change. This will remain true even if change is for the purpose of ensuring that there is enough food to go around, or liberty and justice *for all,* or recognition that when people say they are hurting we are obligated to assume that they may be right.

To be aware of such conditioning is a long way toward liberation from it. But not the full way—the recognition may lead us to retreat even more doggedly into a defensiveness about what we have, no matter how exploitive it may have been to others. It is my fear that such an attitude will overwhelm our national psyche, no matter how much individuals may be liberated from it. We have a preview of what this means in the acceptance in Latin America of the doctrine of *Seguridad Nacionál*, national security: every trend toward change is interpreted as a threat to "national security," every proposal to extend food and shelter and education to those now denied it is seen as a communist plot. Consequently, in the interests of national security any measures are legitimate to thwart the proponents of change, from persuasion to arrest to exile to torture to execution. It is carefully concealed from the people that such "security" is only for the few who have power and want to keep it, and that it really means insecurity for the rest. But since the few have the power and the guns and the prisons, this flaw in the argument can be overlooked.

I am not saying it has come to that in the United States. I am saying that it could. It almost came to that in the McCarthy era, and we were within an inch of it during Watergate. Half an inch. And the more our influence is challenged by the poor of the world, the more our white supremacy is challenged by the non-white majority, the more our "security" is threatened by economic actions of other nations—the more we will be tempted to settle for whatever measures are necessary to keep us on top.

How do we deal with that in a liberating fashion? There is a short answer and a long answer. In a short book, the short answer will have to do. It acknowledges that the doctrine of national security is what the Bible calls "idolatry," which is a fancy name for worshiping a false god. It says that in this case the nation has become a false god, and that that won't work. Whenever we say, "Anything goes . . . " in defending a nation, we have made the nation into the supreme object of our allegiance, and that is what we call a god. Our national temptation, in other words, is never to atheism, but always to polytheism, to the creation of other gods in addition to the true God.

The first commandment prohibits that: "You shall have no other gods before me." This is a very realistic first commandment, since it acknowledges that we are always tempted to create other gods, and that our real problem is one of priorities. The God who spoke the first commandment, the God of the Jews, claims also to be the God of everybody else. Christians affirm the birth of that claim, which means that such a God is the God not only of

Americans but of all people everywhere—Vietnamese, Chileans, Iranians, and Cubans, for example. If "all people everywhere" are the concern of such a God, no segment of that people can declare superiority to the rest, or claim the right to decide unilaterally what is good for them.

This makes it a brand new ball game.

For our day and age, it's the only one worth playing. And the only one that won't destroy us.

13

On Making Friends with Time

It goes with the territory of being a theologian that I am supposed to reflect about life and death, mortality and finitude, time and eternity. I know that death is in store for all of us, but I can usually avoid coming to terms with the fact that it is in store for me.

Even so, I do not here propose to concentrate on death. I propose to concentrate on life—the life that is left to us before death claims us. I do not need death to remind me of the frailty of life, although it certainly helps. All I need is a recognition of the fact that I am growing older, that the number of options open to me is decreasing, that the number of new choices I can make is diminishing rather than expanding, that, in short, many things I want to do will not be able to be done. Damn.

So time has become my enemy. Only recently have I thought of time as an enemy. The catalyst that forced me to confront it was the recognition in 1977, shortly after returning to Union Seminary in what was supposed to be the crowning event of my professional "career," that I was in the wrong job at the wrong time. Rather than faking it out until retirement, as I noted earlier, I decided to resign instead. That left me feeling cleaner, but it also left me unemployed. Any time earlier in my life I would have thought, "Well now, I have two or three chunks of professional life still ahead, what shall I do for the next few years before moving on to something else?" But this time, facing the task of beginning a new job at what would be age fifty-nine, I realized that what I would do for "the next few years" would be my *last* job option. After that, I would (formally at least) "retire." I had one more chance. There is no other realization quite so calculated to transform time into an enemy.

The "job crisis" forced me to look at the whole structure of my life. Maybe other things ought to be reordered as well. I realized that most of the time I live frenetically. I epitomize the hectic pace. Not only do I get overcommitted, I go for long stretches of time doing things I don't really enjoy, for the sake of what may be possible once they are finished. (Catch: They Are Never Finished. Sydney lost her innocence on this matter long ago. She is no longer taken in when she hears me say, very sincerely, "It's going to be less hectic (a) next year, (b) when the book is finished, (c) after I have taught this new course once and am familiar with the material, (d) after the grades are finally in, (e) once the Vietnam War is over, or (f) all of the above.")

But there is more than the hectic pace that makes time an enemy. There is what William Muehl, in a few hard-hitting words, has called " . . . the sudden, keen angry awareness of the frailty of our tenure among all that we have come to love" (*All the Damned Angels,* Pilgrim Press, 1972, p. 100).

That's become the nub of the problem for me. I resent the frailty of my tenure among all that I have come to love. I want it to go on. I want to keep renewing acquaintances with old friends. I want to keep deepening acquaintances with new friends. I want to see Chile free of Pinochet and my exiled friends able to return there. I want to see a birch grove, destroyed by winter ice and my overenthusiastic pruning, reborn from the stumps. I want more years with my wife and children, particularly since those years are getting better all the time. I want to know all the Beethoven string quartets well, and then the piano sonatas. I want to be reassured that political prisoners will be freed. I want to be around when Third-World peoples begin to get their fair shake. *I don't want my tenure among such things to be frail.* And it is. Damn.

John Steinbeck has captured another part of it. In *Sweet Thurdsay,* he introduces a character called Doc, a Chicago Ph.D. who makes his living in Monterey collecting marine specimens from the tide pools and selling them. It's a good life, Doc reflects, but there is also discontent; shivering in the midst of warmth, hunger in the midst of food, yearning in the midst of love.

> And to prod all these there's time, the bastard Time. The end of life is now not so terribly far away—you can see it the way you see the finish line when you come into the stretch—and your mind says, "Have I worked enough? Have I eaten enough? Have I loved enough?" All of these, of course, are the foundation of man's greatest curse, and perhaps his greatest glory. "What has my life meant so far, and what can it mean in the time left to me?" And now we're coming to the wicked, poisoned dart: "What have I contributed to the Great Ledger? What am I worth?" (*Sweet Thursday*, Penguin Books, p. 22)

For Doc, it seems "the bastard Time" finally engenders terror: we are confronted by the Great Ledger with its "wicked, poisoned dart." That part of it does not frighten me as much as it does Doc; perhaps it should frighten me more, perhaps later on it will. Now, at any rate, I believe that what is recorded on the Great Ledger will be weighted on the side of grace and forgiveness, rather than retribution and scorekeeping, and I am content to leave all that to the mercy of God. "What am I worth?" The answer to that question will be given by Another than myself.

What I respond to in the Steinbeck quotation is the sense of time running out: have I lived enough? What can my life mean in the time left to me, which might be very short, since the encroaching years will mean a diminution of my energies—physical, psychic, sexual, mental? With the best will in the world, the most careful regime, my body will slowly run down. It's "the bastard Time" rather than the Great Ledger that has me in its clutches.

Muehl's response is anger, Doc's is at least close to terror. I feel more anger than terror, but more than either anger or terror I feel wistfulness. Wistfulness that it has to be so. Wistfulness that it can't be otherwise. Anger, to be sure, about Chile and political prisoners and injustice to Third-World peoples, but wistfulness about old friends and new friends and family and Beethoven and birch groves.

Would that it were not so. It is so. Damn.

Time. My enemy.

Could the enemy become a friend? Could I make friends with time? Instead of fighting time, could I learn to embrace it? Could I (to stick with Steinbeck's imagery) legitimize the bastard?

I begin to believe that such questions can be answered in the affirmative. But before sharing my gropings in that direction, I want to make an important point, perhaps more important than anything that will follow: *one need not be fifty-nine (as I am) to face these questions and search for answers. The sooner one begins to face them (forty-nine? thirty-nine? twenty-nine? nineteen?) the more time there will be to live out the affirmations toward which they point.* Making friends with time is not an occupation for old folks, it is an occupation for anyone, at any time, who wants life to be fuller rather than emptier.

How, then, legitimize the bastard? As far as my *work life* goes, I'm taking a gamble. I have decided not to defer until "retirement" the thing I think I can do best and most enjoy doing, which is to have some chunks of time for disciplined writing. Up to now my writing has always come between the cracks of other work, sandwiched in between classes, committees, lectures, committees, traveling, committees, causes and committees, and devouring what are laughingly referred to in the family as my "vacations." I want to exercise "an apostolate of the pen" more centrally than I have been able to do so far. So I shall not wait for "retirement" to offer me those chunks of time. I shall claim them right now. This book is the first exercise in my new-found freedom.

It's not quite that simple, of course. I can't simply stop working and start writing. Writers have to eat. They have to provide food for other mouths as well. But I am meeting the problem halfway by cutting back to half-time teaching. I covet that ongoing half-time in the classroom, because I need the stimulus of minds younger than my own to keep me alive, and I profit from the kind of uninhibited critique that twenty-three-year-olds are sometimes willing to offer to fifty-nine-year-olds. Thanks to Pacific School of Religion for sharing in the gamble.

Will it work? Who knows? I may encounter a two-year writing block. I may spend all that "free" time trying to make up for a 50 percent cut in salary. But I may also be unleashed to new creativity. At the moment (and I say this now more bravely than I say it at some other moments) I'm willing to take some actual risks for the sake of some possible gains. Maybe I can make friends with time and we can work together. It's worth a try.

As far as *the rest of my life* goes, I have already made an obvious, though crucial, discovery. It is that although I have zero control over the *quantity* of life still at my disposal (save that I could end it if I chose to do so, and I do not choose to do so), I do have considerable control over the *quality* of time at my disposal. I might live forty more dull and unimaginative years, going through the motions, merely trying to survive and beat the actuarial tables, or I might live four more years, invested with a zest and excitement and fulfillment that would make their relatively short duration much more significant and satisfying than a time span ten times that long.

(I would like, of course, to have the zest and excitement and fulfillment spread out over the forty-year period rather than the four-year period. And even though I have started jogging I probably won't get that wish fulfilled. Damn.)

Where do I go with all that?

Solution: Stop wasting the already precious moments griping about the passage of time and *get on with the affirmation of the present moments as grace-filled.*

A few details of the solution: don't wait for gifts tomorrow, recognize them today since they are all about us. There are times to be redeemed, a world to be transformed, yes; but there are also events to be embraced, little events as well as big ones, and persons to be given affirmation and affection. Although the quantity of those moments is finite, the quality those moments can have is infinite. We embrace them when we affirm the small things that give time its blessed quality—a glance, a sound, a touch, a tiny ritual (the meaning of which perhaps only one other person knows). Such things are complete in themselves. But there is a further blessedness. They not only invest the now with preciousness in its own right, but also they give a new quality to the moments that precede and follow the now—an eternity momentarily glimpsed and forever retrievable through another gift, memory.

It even becomes possible to affirm that the very lessening of the number of such moments is itself beneficent. As long as I presume that I have infinite amounts of time at my disposal, I am likely to squander that time; there will always be another hour or day or week or month or year or decade. But when I realize that the amount of time ahead is limited,

I may be able to use those limited moments more creatively. Their very minuteness adds to their preciousness. What happens during them can have a new depth and intensity, so that they can all become what Evelyn Newman calls "the constant sacrament of the little moment."

To be sure, such an attitude can transform itself into a grim necessity to "make every moment count" in the old frenetic way. If that happens, the sheer abandon that must accompany a true embrace of time may be lost. But recognizing the danger is half the battle in overcoming it. I accept the danger for the sake of the reward beyond the danger.

Christopher Fry (whom I have recently rediscovered) captures this affirmation that the qualitative moments outweigh the quantitative ones, in a comment by Jennet, in *The Lady's Not for Burning* (Oxford University Press, 1959), who falls in love on the night in which she may die:

> What is deep, as love is deep, I'll have
> Deeply. What is good, as love is good,
> I'll have well. Then if time and space
> Have any purpose, I shall belong to it. (p.85)

Another way of making friends with time is to realize that I do not have to "grow old." To be sure, I will "age"—that is irreversible. I will have less physical energy and will have to husband my resources more carefully. But in the process of doing so, I can remember that "aging" can be done with grace rather than bitterness. Dom Helder Camara, who knows about such things, has commented, "A kind old age means growing old on the outside without growing old inside"(de Broucker, *Dom Helder Camera: The Conversions of a Bishop* (Collins, London, 1979, p. 215). Dom Helder is living proof of the truth of his statement. He will never grow old inside.

How does one keep from "growing old inside"? Surely

only in *community*. The only way to make friends with time is to stay friends with people. If I try to deal with time by myself, I lose. Absolutely. Of that I am certain. And I, who tend instinctively to be more of a "private person" than a "public person," need to keep reminding myself of this. A friend of Sydney's and mine, reflecting on the fact that she was happy now in her decision to remain single (she is a successful lawyer), added, rather wistfully and with great perception, "I should like not to grow old alone." Community is of the essence of being human. It will be the more so as we age. Our lawyer friend will find community, even if not the community of marriage.

Taking community seriously not only gives us the companionship we need, it also relieves us of the notion that we are indispensable. What a gift! It is immensely liberating to discover that the world and its future do not depend exclusively on us. Others too can be allowed to help redeem the times. Those who come after us can either build on what we have started, or (as likely) repair the damage we have done. Either way, it is a glorious web of exchange.

Whatever else the Bible means when it talks about the times being "fulfilled," it must also mean that the times are filled full. Filled full not with frenetic rush and haste, not with compulsive activity, but with the things that really count—commitments, causes, work, rest, play, the possibility of change, other selves, incredibly dear persons, laughter, tears, moments that convey beauty, sounds that transmit love.

For all of these I give thanks, acknowledging that they bind my life to others and to the world and thus to God in ways that make my life unimaginably free. And as I give thanks, I must further acknowledge—why did I not see it before?—that *it is time that gives all those things to me.*

Time. My friend.

14

"Theology in a New Key"

The location of this section is the most important thing about it. Not too long ago I would have set out a theology at the *beginning* of the book and then "applied" it to our human situations, as though there were timeless truths arrived at apart from human experience that we first discover and then seek to make relevant. Part of the message of this book is that I now see theology growing out of our struggles; it is our attempt, from a Christian perspective, to think and talk about what has been happening to us. (The word itself, *theo-logy*, the *logos* of *theos*, simply means "discourse about God," or even more simply, "God-talk.") My engagement in concern about civil rights and Vietnam (i.e., the recognition that my globe was shrinking) began to teach me this: reflecting on those experiences, I wrote in 1971, "Theology is formed through engagement instead of detachment, on pavements more than in libraries, and in the midst of ambiguities rather than clarities" (*The Pseudonyms of God,* p. 9). That became true for me. I did not will its truth. It happened . . . and I began to notice what was happening.

The shrinking globe has played havoc with the theology I put together so nicely in seminary and graduate school and my first ten years of teaching. In those days I lived in the world of Anglo-Saxon white theology, spruced up by such continental theology as I could get in translation. (It would never have occured to me in those days that the adjective *continental* could modify any noun save *Europe.*) My French was passable but my German limped. But all was well, for the Scots were turning out translations of Barth's *Dogmatics* faster then I could read them, and Brunner, Bultmann, Berdyaev, Bonhoeffer, and all the other "B's" were available in translations so numerous that I could not have read them all in a lifetime. We were living in an era of giants. Who needed new giants? Our generation's task would be to transmit (possibly in clearer, less technical language) what we had glimpsed while riding on the giants' backs.

How wrong I was.

Most of what I thought of as "normative theology" has turned out to be parochial theology, conditioned by the time and place out of which it arose. Even theologies claiming to be built on "the biblical perspective" turned out to be built on a parochial biblical perspective, i.e., on the Bible as read from a white, male, Western, bourgeois, intellectual perspective. (This happens, I discovered, to be rather different from the perspective of the biblical writers themselves, who usually turn out to have been dark-skinned Orientals, "the poor of the land" rather than the cream of the intelligentsia.)

The recognition that my perspective was just as conditioned as everybody else's, rather than being the "norm" from which "they" (i.e., all those others) deviated, was force-fed to me by the discovery of a shrinking globe, and the recognition that I had been looking and listening in too few places, namely congenial places, close to my geographic and cultural home.

It has meant starting all over again.

An image that has been helpful to me in starting again "in a new key," has been the musical image of the diminished seventh chord, an image I developed in detail in another book, *Theology in a New Key.* In writing music, composers can introduce a chord called the diminished seventh, which enables them to shift abruptly to a new and very different key. This enables them to move arbitrarily in unexpected directions and take their listeners by surprise.

Much the same thing has been happening in theology. We have been singing in a certain key, i.e., North American/European, and now, to our surprise, the song has emerged in a new key sung by a new group of people:

> Many terms have been used to describe these articulators of the theology in a new key—the "wretched of the earth," the poor, the oppressed, the marginalized, the voiceless, the exploited, the victims. Their spokespersons vary and their agendas vary: they are women, blacks, the physically and mentally handicapped, homosexuals, Asians, Latin Americans. Some of them come from Appalachia in West Virginia, others from the antiplano in eastern Peru; some live in the barrios, others in the Bowery; some are at home in Chilean poblaciones, others in Malaysia . . . . their theology is being forged in conversations rather than in academic lectures; printed on mimeographed newssheets (clandestinely distributed with no return address) rather than in volumes selling for $14.95 plus tax; . . . preached in prisons as much as in chapels; sustained by sharing bread in food kitchens rather than refectories; sung in spirituals and blues rather than Bach chorales; celebrated in borrowed clothing rather than in eucharistic vestments; growing out of experiences that gradually become the stuff of theological reflection rather than the other way around. (*Theology in a New Key,* pp. 24-25)

That is the situation out of which the new theology is

emerging. It puts some heavy demands on us, for those perspectives have not been our perspectives, and yet we must respond to them. Two friends, a Protestant and a Jew, have stated the terms of this response. Here is an iconoclastic fellow Presbyterian, John Fry (*The Great Apostolic Blunder Machine*, Harper & Row, 1978, pp. 174-75): "I propose that theologians write theology from the standpoint of the mother in Bombay (or Pittsburgh) whose child has just starved to death. She would not be theology's primary reader, and her situation would not provide theology's subject matter. [But] her rage and grief would provide its angle of vision."

Alongside that I put a searing statement by Rabbi Irving Greenberg, who—writing after the holocaust in which six million Jews (including one and one half million children) died in the crematoria of eastern Europe—offers a new "working principle" for the future: "No statement, theological or otherwise, should be made that would not be credible in the presence of burning children."

I do not know any words more challenging to the theological enterprise today than those, though I acknowledge that they virtually ordain muteness: *what* statement about meaning or purpose or hope would "be credible in the presence of burning children"? I will many times (not least within the pages of this book) be faithless to those two injunctions, but I intend from now on to try to be responsive to their stern demands.

This means that the problems of faith today are no longer so much *academic* (the mind/body problem, the relationship of freedom and necessity, the anomaly of God's existence in the world of modern science, the relationship of prayer and autosuggestion) as they are *human-social*. (Why does faith not empower people to change? How can we contain the forces of evil? Where is love in a world of burning or starving children? Why are we so reluctant to side with the poor?) Are the latter questions "ethical" or "theological"?

Our shrinking globe has fuzzed the line between ethics and theology. Am I a "theological ethicist" or an "ethical theologian"? That is the number one nonquestion on my personal agenda.

Both Fry and Greenberg make the fate of children a starting point for theological reflection. To be sure, Dostoyevsky said that with passion also. But I hear Fry and Greenberg even more passionately since they are writing today. And I propose to accept their converging testimony as defining the moral criterion for future theology: *it must be a theology that puts the welfare of children above the niceties of metaphysics.* Any theology that provides for the creative growth of children will make it on all other scores. A card from a friend in Chile states the goal of those temporarily forced underground by the Pinochet regime: "Y los únicos privilegiados seran los niños" ("and the only privileged ones will be the children"). A fit description of the kingdom of God.

But theology in a new key will not only reflect on what is going on; it will do so in the light of a history of Christian reflection and experience. The signpost of that heritage has been the Scriptures. But there is a problem. The Scriptures have frequently laid a baleful hand on fresh movements of the Spirit, stifling them by sanctions drawn from an era long past. Even so, a "rereading" of the Scriptures is going on in our day, particularly in situations of oppression, out of which the biblical message is reinforcing the need for change rather than sanctioning ongoing repression. A series of sixty-six books that came out of situations of oppression are once again offering good news of liberation from that oppression—whether psychic, political, social, or economic. They are communicating a message that centuries of Western bourgeois interpretation had skillfully covered over. (Recall the "verbal snapshot" from Lima, Peru.) The phenomenon is showing us how much we need to be freed from the ideological blinders of our North American/European upbringing.

The Bible was originally a revolutionary book ("good news to the *poor* . . . ").

We tamed it.

And now our sisters and brothers in the Third-World are freeing it up once again to communicate its liberating message.

We used to take account of how the Bible was read (by the critics) in Tübingen or Marburg.

Now we must take account of how the Bible is read (by the practitioners) in Solentiname or Soweto.

Two different Bibles emerge, depending on the perspective from which the one Bible is read. One perspective very skillfully justifies Western bourgeois capitalist culture. That is the comforting Bible we have read. The other challenges all the assumptions of that culture and offers the ingredients for creating an alternative world. Something about the kingdom of God being like a little child. . . ("And the only privileged ones will be the children.")

So, out of reflection on what is going on in a world of injustice, and in the light of a biblical promise of liberation from injustice, a new theology is emerging. Different people are doing it in different ways. Three points of special emphasis are emerging for me, each enriching and informing the others. One is geographical, a second is historical and cultural, a third is methodological. Here is that agenda, set out with telegraphic brevity:

1. The geographical ingredient that must be taken with utmost seriousness is the voice of *the Third-World*. For me, Latin America has been the focal point, but similar currents are at work in Asia and Africa as well. Indeed, to be open to "the voice of the Third-World" means to be open to those near at hand as well, who are dispossessed and exploited, whether for racist, sexist, or cultural reasons. Theologies that fail to hear the cries of the hurting, and fail in their responses to seek to alleviate the need for those cries, are no longer theologies worthy of attention.

2. The particular historical-cultural ingredient to which theology in a new key must respond is *post-holocaust Judaism*. Indeed, Christians need to listen to Judaism as a whole, since our historical record *vis-a-vis* Judaism, is worse than our record with any other faith—a devastating indictment. We have killed, tortured, manipulated, proselytized, and discriminated against Jews in ways and to a degree that are the shame of our history. And all of this is brought to pinpoint focus in the event of the holocaust, and what Christians do about it in a postholocaust era. The deliberate murder of six million Jews by those who were Christians, or were at least shaped by an ostensibly Christian culture, makes forever impossible some of our previous theological assertions about (a) the inherent goodness of human nature, (b) a universe in which "all things work together for good," (c) any equations between justice and virtue, or (d) just about anything else. A pall is forever cast over complacent or triumphant orthodoxies. There is little of past Christian theology, let us face it, that is "credible in the presence of burning children." Massive overhaul is called for here, not only substantively but sensitively: a new theological modesty about what we can actually say, coupled with humility and penitence in the face of our corporate complicity in past evil and our individual and corporate complicity in ongoing evil.

3. The methodological ingredient of the new theology is *story*. Our faith does not come to us initially as theology, and particularly not as "systematic theology," but as story. Tell me about God: "Well, once upon a time there was a garden . . . " Tell me about Jesus: "Once upon a time there was a boy in a little town in Palestine called Nazareth . . . ." Tell me about salvation: "Well, when the same boy grew up, he loved people so much that the rulers began to get frightened of him, and you know that they did? . . ." Tell me about the church: "Well, there were a great many people who worked together: Mary and Priscilla and

Catherine of Siena and Martin Luther and Martin Luther King, Jr., and John (several Johns: John Calvin, John Knox, John XXIII) and Gustavo and Sister Theresa, and you know what they did? . . ."

Out of such stories, systems begin to grow. The growing is loss, not gain. Stories about a garden become cosmological arguments; stories about Jesus become treatises on the two natures; stories about salvation become substitutionary doctrines of atonement; stories about the church become bylaws of male-domination hierarchies. Who could care less?

In losing the story we have lost the power and therefore the glory. Theologians bear a large measure of responsibility for this. We have committed the unpardonable sin of transforming exciting stories into dull systems. We have spawned system after system: Augustinian, Anselmian, Thomistic, Calvinistic, Lutheran, Reformed, orthodox, liberal, neoorthodox, neoliberal. Historically they were very different; today they share in common an inability to grab us where we are and say, "Listen! This is important!"

We must *recover the story* if we are to recover a faith for our day. Each of us has his or her story. Alongside them is the Christian story, a story of the heroes and heroines of faith. Could the pair of stories impact one another? Sometimes we hear another person's story, either in biography or fiction, and we say, "Aha! That's *my* story too. In learning about Abraham Lincoln and Jane Addams and Frodo Baggins I am learning about myself." Our theological task is to find ways to "tell the old, old story" so that the listener says, "Aha! That's *my* story too! In learning about Abraham and Deborah and Jesus (and Judas) I am learning about myself." I think there are ways to begin to do it, but that is an assignment for a later book, and, I fear, a larger one—the second exercise of my new-found freedom.

I suggested earlier that the three approaches are interrelated. It is story that is the interrelating factor.

Third-World Christians reflect on their situation of oppression and the need for liberation; they reread the biblical story of people under oppression who are liberated, and find their present story being informed and guided by the ancient one. So the Exodus story becomes their story. What was good news back then (liberation from past oppression) can become good news once again (liberation from present oppression). They are discovering that the biblical story is not just a story about "way back then," but their own story as well, firmly planted in "here and now."

A similar thing has been happening with postholocaust Jewish attempts to recover a sense of identity after all identity had been stripped away. Elie Wiesel's writings are a telling example. In half a dozen novels he has explored what it means to be a Jew living in a world in which Auschwitz could take place. The stories at first were very contemporary. But soon the eighteenth and nineteenth century Hasidic tales began to be woven in. Then even earlier Midrashic commentary on Scripture made its appearance. Recently he has been retelling tales from the Hebrew Scriptures. None of this is a retreat into the past. It is an attempt *to understand the present by making use of the past.* In retelling the ancient tales, Wiesel informs us, he is coming to understand who he is today. The old story becomes his story.

Both Third-World theologians and postholocaust Jews have been recovering stories from the past that lead to a new understanding of their own stories in the present. The convergence is too marked to be capricious. It suggests the appropriate theological task for Christians in the future: to explore the ways that stories are told, all kinds of stories, to see if that could help us uncover a way of retelling the Christian story so that listeners, confronted by such retelling, could say, "Aha! That's my story too!"

Once we have done that, there will be plenty of time to worry about systems.

15

The Saving Grace of Humor; or,

The Eighth Gift of the Spirit

We all know that seven is a very mystical number. There are seven deadly sins. And, perhaps to compensate, there are seven gifts of the Spirit. Isaiah describes them:

> the spirit of wisdom and understanding,
> the spirit of counsel and might,
> the spirit of knowledge and the fear of the Lord. (11:2)

Even superficial scrutiny will indicate that Isaiah catalogs only six gifts of the spirit. My own theory is that when Jerome translated the Old Testament from Hebrew into Latin (the Vulgate), he added a seventh gift, piety, in his translation of the above passage, because as we all know, seven is a very mystical number, and it would be more seemly for the Spirit to bequeath seven gifts rather than six, especially in the light of the seven deadly sins that need to be overcome.

I am sufficiently impressed with Jerome's addition to
Isaiah's text to emulate him and add yet another to the gifts
of the Spirit, even though it means forfeiting the mystical
number seven. For I believe that there is an eighth gift of
the Spirit: it is the saving grace of humor.

By "the saving grace of humor" I do not mean primarily
the ability to "be funny," though that helps. I regret
introducing such a qualification, since I think that being
funny is one of the nicest things people do. But a sense of
humor, as I will use it, has to do with *seeing things in proper
proportion,* which means (among other things) having an
appropriately modest view of ourselves, since we usually
view ourselves with disproportionate immodesty. The
saving grace of humor, then, is not only an ability to laugh,
but (most savingly, most grace-fully) an ability to laugh *at
ourselves.* It involves a willingness to be cut down to size and
emerge liberated rather than devastated by the experience.

(Interestingly enough, the medieval physiological understanding of "humor" underlines this modern use of the
word. "Humor" was one of the four elemental fluids of the
body—blood, phlegm, and black and yellow bile being the
others—which were "regarded as determining, *by their
relative proportions,* a person's physical and mental constitu-
tion.")

Let me illustrate this matter of seeing ourselves in a new
light as a result of the saving grace of humor. A number of
years ago I preached in Buffalo, New York. It was a
double-service situation: run through the liturgy at 9:30,
have a quick cup of coffee, go to the bathroom, and then do
the same thing again at 11. Before my 9:30 sermon I was
prayed over by the local parson (an experience that always
leaves me nervous anyhow): ". . . O Lord, grant unto thy
servant with us this morning a portion of thy grace, that he
may rightly divide the word of truth." Fair enough, I decided,
despite my nervousness; I need all the help I can get.

Then the local parson heard my sermon.

At the 11 o'clock service, he repeated everything he had said in the earlier service, word for word, phrase for phrase, pause for pause, save that when he came to the portion of his prayer quoted above, he escalated the petition: ". . . O Lord, grant unto thy servant with us this morning a *double* portion of thy grace. . . "

That story is always good for a laugh, but to me it is more than an attention-getter at the start of a talk—a use to which I have put it on more occasions than I care to divulge. For the incident did serve, and continues to serve, as a creative way of cutting me down to size, of restoring a sense of porportion about just where I rate on a scale of homiletical attainments. I came, I preached, and the local pastor's assessment of my effort was, "My God, man! You not only need help, you need extra help." Whenever I am tempted to pretentiousness, to thinking of myself more highly than I ought to think, to spiritual complacency or (worse) stuffiness, The Buffalo Prayer (as I have come to call it) is on hand to restore a true sense of proportion. I avail myself almost daily of its therapeutic power.

Humor at its best, then, serves to help us keep things in proportion. We think we have life all doped out, that we understand how things fit together, that we know our own strengths and weaknesses—and then an unexpected incongruity presents itself, in a joke or an experience or an aside, and we realize that we are *not* so much in control of things as we thought we were . . . whether the joke is on us or not. For even when the joke is not on us, we are reminded, by the unexpected juxtapositions leading to the punch line, that *we didn't know what the punch line was going to be.*

That's a healthy, leveling experience for smug, assured people. We have been fooled. We are less (and more) than we thought we were. Life is more incongruous than we imagined. There is more unexpectedness, more mystery, than we had bargained for. If the Archbishop of Canterbury slips on a banana peel on the way to his coronation, we laugh because of the incongruity; Archbishops and banana peels don't belong in the same sentence or even the same paragraph, and yet there they are right smack together in Real Life, confounding us. If, to boot, the Archbishop of Canterbury is a creature of enormous girth (which can almost be guaranteed), the incongruity between pompous dignity and human frailty is further enhanced, and we laugh more loudly. In any case, we recover a better sense of proportion. Dignified processions are not immune from comic disaster. A splendid discovery! We will never again be quite so impressed with dignified processions. Kierkegaard once remarked how comic it was that the philosopher Hegel, who had managed to contain the whole universe within a single, rationally comprehensible system, should occasionally be obliged to turn aside and sneeze.

Not all humor is kind, not even the above humor (as the Archbishop of Canterbury and the philosopher Hegel would be the first to agree). But there is a yet deeper constriction on humor. Christians, for example, don't joke about the crucifixion of Jesus. And nobody is entitled to joke about Jews in Nazi concentration camps. When people attempt either exercise, we call their humor "sick." For on Golgotha and in Treblinka, the incongruities are already (and the word is carefully chosen) painfully apparent.

Humor at the expense of someone else also lacks saving grace. Only Jews are really entitled to tell "Jewish jokes." When others do, a knife is usually being wielded. Ditto for Poles. I may joke about my own pain (if I am able), but I may not joke about the pain of another. Banter, as a form of humor, is double-edged, for the same reason. It takes two people sure enough of themselves to withstand a raillery that always borders on hurting rather than healing. I happen to enjoy exchanges that go by the name of "friendly banter," and with someone (like a Bill Coffin) who can give as good as he gets, spoofing can be creative. But a spoof can easily slide into something snide. The dictionary reminds us that secondary synonyms for "banter" are teasing, ridiculing, deriding, and mocking. Any humor that can be so described is likely to be a tool of oppression rather than a vehicle of liberation.

Humor can also be threatening. If our own pretensions are too openly unmasked by someone else, we feel exploited, and our laughter may be an uneasy cover-up for acute discomfort. There is a nervous laughter that betrays our insecurity more than it signals our ready acceptance of a new (and probably demoted) status. We all experience how laughter and tears can dissolve on a moment's notice into each other, quite beyond our control. Clowns make us laugh, but clowns are often caught in pathetic, if not tragic, situations, and when we laugh at them, it is partly out of relief that they, rather than we, are in the situation where no release from frustration is possible.

So humor, like all things, is ambiguous. And in this it is not unlike faith. For, as Reinhold Niebuhr frequently pointed out, both humor and faith deal with the incongruities of our existence. Humor, he says concerns the *immediate* incongruities (the juxtaposition of archbishop and banana peel or the fact that Hegel should have to sneeze), whereas faith concerns the *ultimate* incongruities (that the same person should both have a vision of eternal life and yet be mortal, or that sinful, corrupt creatures should nevertheless be loved and forgiven by their Creator). In both cases, the amazing thing is that we are able, to some degree, to stand outside of ourselves and see ourselves more clearly than would otherwise be possible (what Neibuhr calls "transcending our immediacy," if that is any help).

Humor helps us to see how incongruous it is that we make infinite claims about ourselves when we are only finite creatures; faith helps us see how incongruous it is that infinite claims should be made on our behalf by Another.

And yet the fact that they are made anyhow, and that they finally define who we are, blesses the incongruity. That we should be loved by One greater than we are, is the ultimate incongruity. To believe it is to be able to indulge in laughter—not the laughter of nervousness or the laughter of being unmasked, but the laughter of pure joy that despite everything, it should be so.

That it *is* so, frees us from having to take ourselves seriously, which is a truly saving grace. The greatest thing about Karl Barth is not that he wrote twelve volumes of *Church Dogmatics* within a single lifetime, but that he was content to leave the project unfinished and not feel cheated. He knew how pretentious it would be for any mortal, even one of the stature of Karl Barth, finally to wipe the ink off his hands and say, "That completes it. I have now captured the essence of divinity within the compass of thirteen volumes."

With a measure of insight rarely granted theologians, Barth once wrote:

> The angels laugh at old Karl. They laugh at him because he tries to grasp the truth about God in a book of Dogmatics. They laugh at the fact that volume follows volume and each is thicker than the previous one. As they laugh, they say to one another, "Look! Here he comes now with his little pushcart full of volumes of the Dogmatics!" And they laugh about the men who write so much about Karl Barth instead of writing about the things he is trying to write about. Truly, the angels laugh.

To the degree that such an attitude could be appropriated by others, it would be my wish that every future theologian be a "Barthian." It is almost enough to make one believe in angels.

I have spoken of humor as a gift of the Spirit. Why a gift? Because we are not likely to initiate actions that will cut us down to size, deflating us to a proper sense of proportion about who we are. That will never be something we seek.

But it is something we can receive, w
gift, even if not a gift for which
thankful. How many will initially rejo
we are less significant than we supp
And yet, if we are, in fact, less signific
ourselves to be, it is surely to our bene
rather than to live out of a false perce
or later betray us.

And here a paradox emerges. For to discover that our
own pretensions need to be destroyed and that we are not
quite as lovely as we thought we were, and *then* to discover
that we are the recipients of divine love even so, meaning
that we are infinitely *more* significant than we could ever
have imagined before—that is a gift worth having.

And it is not only a gift, it is a gift of the Spirit. I'm not
quite sure what it means to say this, save that it must mean a
gift coming from God and therefore ultimately good, both
in intent and content. I believe there is a grace that is willing
to chide us gently about our pretensions, and does so more
forcefully if we resist the gentle chiding, until we have had
stripped away from us whatever blinds our eyes, seals our
ears, and warps our wills.

Then, perhaps, we can begin to know, even as we are
known.

16

Beauty and the Oppressed

There is beauty and there are the humiliated. Whatever difficulties the enterprise may present, I would like never to be unfaithful either to the one or the other.—Camus, a second time

For Camus, the ")ifficulties" presented by the enterprise of relating beauty and the oppressed never went away. His concern is stated in an early essay, and he was still wrestling with it at the time he died. I'm sure I will be too.

But I have been able to affirm something that Camus rejects. I can best get at it through a very simple Christmas carol. It contains an invitation to "All Poor Folk and Humble" to come to the Bethlehem stable. They are not to feel afraid, "for Jesus our Treasure, with love past all measure, in lowly poor manger was laid." Poor folk, humble folk, crude surroundings, makeshift crib, child of poor and oppressed people. There is the oppression side of it laid out clearly.

But as the carol continues and the poor present their gifts, there is an unexpected line: ". . .and Jesus in *beauty*, accepted their duty." There is the beauty side of it laid out equally clearly.

That unexpected juxtaposition of beauty and the oppressed in the Bethlehem stable is very important to me. I believe that God's act of sending love into the world in Jesus of Nazareth is an act of great *beauty*, since beauty and love can never be far apart. But I also believe that from the very first, and up to the very last, the beauty was expressed in the form of identification with the oppressed. "From the very first": the birthplace was a stable, not a villa or a hospital or a penthouse; transposed to our time it would have been a garage and probably a crummy one at that. "Up to the very last": the death place was the city garbage dump, reserved for the execution of criminals. (Let the Isenheim altarpiece of Grünewald, with its grisly, green-tinted Jesus, stand as the final refutation of any notion that the beauty represented there was "attractive.") Yes, it is love identified with the oppressed, this beauteous love of which the carol sings. *Beauty and the oppressed come together in the Jesus story.*

There was corroboration of this for me in those Jewish faces I saw at Beth Hatefutsoth. They were instances of beauty sprinkled across aeons of oppression, and there are similar instances of beauty today in Chimbote and Rimac and wherever the Pepos of this world are active. Such faces may be sufficient to persuade many people that beauty and the oppressed do come together. But for me, as a Christian, the face of Jesus (which I have never seen but must now look for in the faces of the poor) is the crowning instance of this truth, and I must testify to it.

This means that Camus and the Christian have different questions. For Camus, the question is; How can beauty and the oppressed be understood together? For the Christian, the question is; How could they possibly be understood separately?

The evidence converges wherever we turn. Hear the Jesus story through Bach's *B Minor Mass,* one of the supreme expressions of beauty in all human history. As we are drawn into its world of reverence and penitence and awe, we are confronted not only with Bach's skill as a creator of beauty, but also with his faith in God, as his music mediates God's reality to us. But what kind of God does it mediate? Not a God who is aloof and self-complete, but a God who is present for us *(Et Incarnatus Est)* in the form of the oppressed one, despised, rejected, and put to death *(Et Sepultus Est),* the one who does the dirty, messy job of bearing the sins of the world, as the *Qui Tollis Peccata Mundi* so breathtakingly illustrates.

In this case—and, I increasingly believe, in every other case—to be confronted by beauty is also to be confronted by the oppressed. They cannot be separated. Why not? *Because God is a God whose beauty is communicated to us through the oppressed one.* When we sing to God, "Tis only the splendor of light hideth thee," we can do so only because we have already been confronted by that God in a human life about whom it was said prospectively that "he was despised and rejected by men; a man of sorrows, and acquainted with grief" (Isa. 53:3*a*). Beauty . . . oppression.

So I conclude that concern for beauty is not a moral copout. It leads us firmly into the midst of all that is going on in our world. Where there is beauty apparent, we are to enjoy it; where there is beauty hidden, we are to unveil it; where there is beauty defaced, we are to restore it; where there is no beauty at all, we are to create it. All of which places us, too, in the arena where oppression occurs, where the oppressed congregate, and where we too are called to be.

Conclusion:

The Precariousness of Prognostication;
or
"To Everything There Is a Season,"
But Sometimes It's Hard
To Read the Weather Map Correctly
or
On Learning to Live with Ambiguity
*(A conclusion in which the title
is almost as long as the text)*

Another time of dislocation is beginning. Sidney and I start new jobs in a new place. There will be new colleagues, new schedules, a new tempo. Thank God we have each other.

Who can tell whether this dislocation will be creative or not? The evidence is not yet in. It is only beginning to accumulate. The moments of grace are better discerned retrospectively than prospectively, though sometimes *(fantastic* grace) we realize at the moment what is happening—that this is a climax, or a turning point, or a new beginning, and that it is grace-filled. Most of the time we know this only in retrospect. We look back and we say, "Aha! *That* was when things began to clarify, or empowerment came, or a weight began to be lifted." Very seldom can we structure such moments ahead of time. That would mean that we were manipulating them (and those involved in them) rather than being transformed by them. We must live with the possibility that decisions made in good faith will turn out to be disasters. If so, then the movement of grace will consist in providing enough power to turn even a disaster toward good and useful ends.

So in the midst of uncertainty about the future, I do not feel abandoned. I feel upheld, even though I have to remind myself from time to time that there is a power beyond myself doing the upholding.

The particular story that I have been telling does not end with a tidy conclusion. In fact, it does not end at all. That is the nature of the Christian story, too. It goes on. The book is never finished. We simply begin a new chapter. That is why the journey is occasionally terrifying, sometimes fulfilling, and always exciting.

Stories that are neatly drawn together on the final page are the exception, not the rule. So I am only articulating, by my own story, the experience of every human being. For all of us, future dislocations loom, whether their content is job insecurity, spiritual spentness, the fear of death, the loss of familiar surroundings and dear friends, or the sheer tedium of a humdrum life. And I affirm, in the face of all that, that the dislocations can be given creative content, not just because we determinedly will it so, but because we are sustained by grace, whether we call it that or not.

So hail to the dislocations. May they be grace-filled. Blessed be their name.